Ancient Peoples and Places

THE PICTS

General Editor

DR. GLYN DANIEL

ABOUT THE AUTHOR

A native of Scotland, Isabel Henderson holds a Master of Arts degree from the University of Aberdeen. At Cambridge University, where she earned a doctorate in 1961, she was a Carnegie Trust Scholar and a Research Fellow of Newnham College. Dr. Henderson is a frequent contributor of articles on the Picts to learned journals, and is currently an Assistant Keeper in the Printed Books Department of the National Library of Scotland in Edinburgh.

Ancient Peoples and Places

THE PICTS

Isabel Henderson

65 PHOTOGRAPHS
32 LINE DRAWINGS
8 MAPS

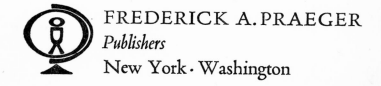

FREDERICK A. PRAEGER
Publishers
New York · Washington

THIS IS VOLUME FIFTY-FOUR IN THE SERIES

Ancient Peoples and Places

GENERAL EDITOR: DR. GLYN DANIEL

BOOKS THAT MATTER

Published in the United States of America in 1967
by Frederick A. Praeger, Inc., Publishers
111, Fourth Avenue, New York, N.Y. 10003
© Isabel Henderson 1967
Library of Congress Catalog Card Number: 67–15744
Printed in Holland

CONTENTS

5

ILLUSTRATIONS

Preface

THE PICTS have acquired the reputation of being quite the darkest of the peoples of Dark Age Britain. As the formidable enemies of the Romans swarming over Hadrian's Wall the Picts are familiar enough, but before and after this break in the clouds all is obscure and what people remember best about the Picts is that very little is known about them. Virtually no Pictish records have survived and modern scholars can still not provide neat answers to such basic questions as, who they were, what language they spoke, what they called themselves and what happened to them after the Scots took over. There is a large corpus of Pictish monumental art of high quality but it is unfortunate that even here, where the advocate for the interest and importance of the Picts has his strongest case, there should be prominently displayed on these sculptures an elaborate but quite unintelligible symbolism. It is scarcely surprising therefore, that the Picts are commonly regarded, even in Scotland, as a peculiar, probably backward, people who have failed to make an adequate mark on history.

This popular verdict has not deterred scholars. The Picts have provided the Scottish antiquarian with quite his happiest hunting ground. Where the facts are so few theories have abounded and the ingenuity and industry expended upon them limitless. A writer in 1927 remarked on 'the almost morbid interest with which the Picts have been regarded in recent times', and in 1947, an Irishman admittedly, diagnosed the disease of 'Pictomania'.

Behind the many bitter controversies on particular problems much solid work has been accomplished and I wish to acknowledge here my dependence upon the work of earlier writers. W. F. Skene's three-volume narrative history: *Celtic Scotland* (1876–

1880) still provides a useful framework for the period even although parts of it have had to be modified by later specialist studies. It is not, I think, going too far to say that an account of the Picts could not be written at all without the aid of the first volume of A. O. Anderson's *Early Sources of Scottish History* (1922). For the first chapter of this book I have made much use of the collection of specialist essays edited by Dr F. T. Wainwright under the well-chosen title, *The Problem of the Picts* (1955). This collection marks a turning point in Pictish studies, for, as Dr Wainwright wrote in his preface, 'We were surprised again and again to find that our different approaches were leading to the same conclusions. A few minor divergences of opinion remain, but they are quite overshadowed by the overwhelming weight of our agreement. This is a new thing among students of the Picts...'.

Pictish studies, far from being a worked-out seam, as is often supposed, are at present in a hopeful and thriving condition. On the historical side a new edition of the most important source, the lists of the Pictish kings, is in preparation, and the archaeologists' recent advances in the definition of the Scottish Iron Age are bound to cast light on the early history of the Picts. The first identifications for a genuinely Pictish archaeology have been made and place-name evidence is in the process of being re-collected and reconsidered.

Nevertheless it is perhaps as well to admit from the outset that not only is there a great deal which is not known about the Picts but also that, in all probability, there is much that will never be known. The only native written record which has survived is a list of kings with their reign lengths – the most primitive of all historical records. There are no surviving Pictish laws, annals, charters, *Lives* of native saints, Calendars, Martyrologies, or collections of native stories and verse. These gaps are in themselves enormous, and to them must be added the greatest gap of all, the lack of a single complete sentence written in the Pictish language. The Pictish personality is therefore utterly lost to us. All the things which give contemporary Ireland and Wales their special character and charm, and which make it possible, even at this distance in time, to comprehend something of the particular sensibilities of these Celtic peoples could, only by the most unlikely chance, be recovered for the Picts.

The exception to this, of course, is the work of the Pictish sculptors, which provides our only contact with the Pictish mentality. Their art is distinctive and forceful and thoroughly conversant with contemporary achievements in the field. Pictish art looks like the product of a sensitive, aware, intelligent society with an individual note of its own, indications which make the loss of its laws, literature and scholarship something of a tragedy.

The Carnegie trust for the Universities of Scotland made me a generous grant towards the cost of illustrating this book. The Trust also financed both my research on Pictish sources and on Pictish art, and I am glad to have the opportunity here of acknowledging my deep indebtedness to them.

My special thanks are due also to Mr R.B.K. Stevenson, Keeper of the National Museum of Antiquities of Scotland, who gave much help with photographs and who supervised my work on Pictish art.

My chief debt is to Mrs Nora K. Chadwick, who first introduced me to the problems of the Picts and who, with all her vast experience and insight, skilfully guided my work on them in Cambridge. I am proud to be one of the many who have received her unstinted support, inspiration and friendship.

I.H.

CHAPTER I

The Formation of the Kingdom of the Picts

THE NORTHERN TRIBES

PICTI was the name given by Classical writers from the late third century AD to the tribes in the far north who, along with the *Scotti* from the west, invaded the Roman province of Britain. Its origin is uncertain, but for the Romans it was a useful collective name for the heterogeneous tribes north of the Forth-Clyde estuaries. The use of 'Pictish' must therefore be reserved for periods later than AD 300 and what goes before must be described as 'proto-Pictish', or better perhaps, '*Pritenic*', from *Priteni*, the name used by the Roman Britons for the northern peoples and which appears in Irish vernacular sources as *Cruithni*.

Fig. 1

Recent authoritative accounts of the *Pritenic* and late Roman period of the northern tribes have appeared in two volumes of Dr F. T. Wainwright's *Studies in History and Archaeology*. The subject of the present book is the mainstream of Pictish history but this chapter will deal briefly with some of this background material and with certain specialist matters such as language, social customs and territorial divisions, which have always taken a central place in Pictish Studies but which belong in origin to this early period.

The most important source for the tribal make-up of the pre-historic Pictish area is Ptolemy's map of Great Britain, compiled from sources of the first century AD. Ptolemy orientated the northern half of the island wrongly but apart from this the map is perfectly recognizable. The names of special interest in this connection lie to the corrected north of Ptolemy's *clotae aestuarium* (the Firth of Clyde) and the *Boderiae aestuarium* (the Firth of Forth). From the extract from his map shown here it can be seen that what was to become the main Pictish area, bounded

Fig. 2

by the Moray Firth, the Great Glen and the Forth-Clyde line, was in the hands of four tribes: the *Caledonii, Vacomagi, Taezali* and *Venicones*.

It is possible to locate these central tribes more precisely by identifying the place-names and natural features associated with their names on the unabridged map. The *Caledonii* occupy the territory running from the Beauly Firth to Perthshire, where traces of their name still survive in place-names such as Dun-keld and Schiehallion. The *Caledonii* must have formed a large well-organized tribe, able to turn to its advantage the water-ways and passes of its central mountainous region. Professor Ian Richmond argued that the placing of the *Vacomagi* on the map may have depended on the placing of *Pinnata Castra,* and if this, as is probable, represents the Roman fort at Inchtuthil, at the southern end of Strathmore, then the misplacing of the fort on the shores of the Moray Firth distorted the location of the tribe in whose territory it was known to lie. The true home of the *Vacomagi* may therefore lie along Strathmore, the district from the Tay to the Dee which was of such importance in the period of the historical Picts. The *Taezali*, through whose ter-ritory flows the river *Deva*, the Dee, belong to Aberdeenshire. The *Venicones* are placed firmly between the Firths of Tay and Forth and the associated place-name *Orrea* has been identified as the Roman fort at Carpow on the south side of the Tay estuary.

If these locations are correct, then the appearance of what was to become the main Pictish area about five hundred years later is of a central band running from south to north occupied by the *Caledonii* and of three coastal groups on the east, the *Veni-cones,* the *Vacomagi* and the *Taezali*.

In his account of the Severan campaigns at the beginning of the third century, Cassius Dio, a contemporary historian, states that the country north of the Forth-Clyde wall was in the hands of the *Caledonii* and the *Maeatae*, two tribes whom he describes

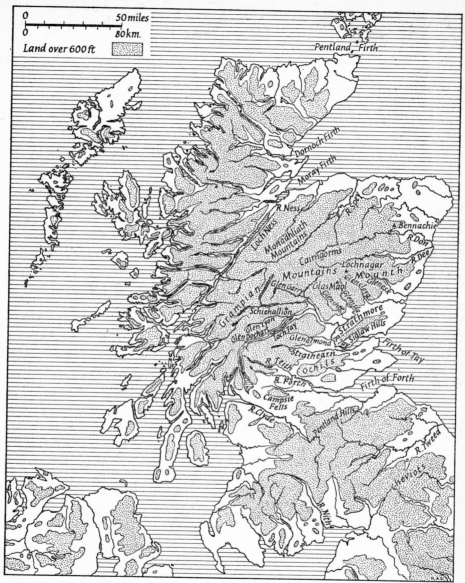

Fig. 1. Physical map of Scotland

17

as 'the greatest peoples', who had absorbed all the other tribes. According to Dio the *Maeatae* lived close to the wall, the *Caledonii* beyond them. From his account of their dealings with the Romans it is clear that the two tribes considered themselves entirely independent of one another.

It is likely that the territory referred to is the main Pictish area and that Ptolemy's four tribes had formed into two confederacies. The *Caledonii* are presumably made up of Ptolemy's tribe of that name, and if the confederacy called the *Maeatae* lived near the Antonine Wall, then it must presumably comprise the *Vacomagi* of Strathmore and the *Venicones* of Fife now spread into Stirlingshire. The alignment of the *Taezali* is uncertain.

Writing in the second half of the fourth century, the historian Ammianus Marcellinus states quite specifically that the Picts are divided into two peoples, the *Dicalydones* and *Verturiones*. Again it seems likely that the first name represents the *Caledonii,* but it can only be assumed that the *Verturiones* are the *Maeatae,* who were presumably originally the *Venicones* and *Vacomagi.* Whilst Professor T. F. O'Rahilly offered as a firmer basis for these identifications the suggestion that *Venicones* could be a manuscript corruption for *Verturiones,* Professor K. H. Jackson has drawn attention to an inscription which proves that *Venicones* is a correct form, so that we are left with the unsatisfactory chain of assumptions given above.

What seems clear is that from the second to the fourth century the main Pictish area was divided into two politically, and it has been suggested that these two divisions, despite changes of name, remained static as political conceptions with the Mounth as the barrier between the two. The natural barrier of the Mounth must always, of course, have imposed a degree of separation upon the tribes on either side of it, but it is well supplied with passes. As the evidence stands, the line of division might equally well have run up the middle of the country, with the *Caledonii* on the west and the three coastal tribes on the east.

Plate 10

18

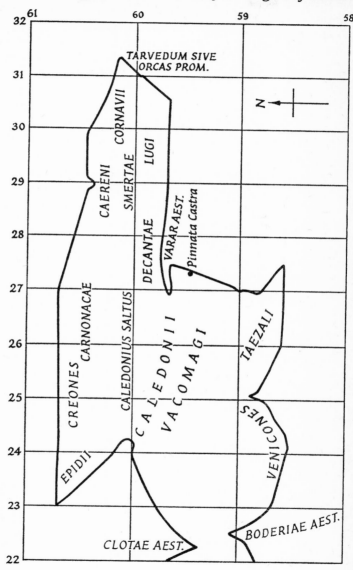

Fig. 2. Extract from Ptolemy's Map of North Britain. (Taken from the explanatory leaflet to the map of Roman Britain published by the Ordnance Survey)

PRE-PICTISH STRUCTURES

The view has been expressed that Pictish archaeology as such can scarcely be said to exist, and in the sense that structures and finds which can confidently be associated with the historical Picts are meagre, this is so. On the other hand recent archae-ological advances in the elucidation of the Celtic settlement of the Pictish area in the Bronze and, particularly, the early Iron Age have been considerable, and in time this must begin to open up whole new vistas of the earliest part of the Pictish historical period. At the moment archaeologists tend to refer cautiously to a post-broch, pre-Viking period, carefully avoid-ing the label 'Pictish' which has been so abused in the past. In the old days brochs and *souterrains* were known as Picts' castles and Picts' houses. But brochs and *souterrains* cannot be called Pictish for they belong to a period before the emergence of the historical Picts and are not even found exclusively in districts which later comprised part of the historical kingdom of the Picts. Nevertheless, the builders of these and other contempor-ary structures were, in all probability, the ancestors of at least some elements in the Pictish population and so require mention here, if only in very general terms.

It has been shown that from about 100 BC two settlements occurred in the north. These were basically refugee movements, due to Roman pressure in Gaul and South Britain. The routes taken to the north cannot be determined with absolutely cer-tainty but it seems that at least one element in the north-western settlement made contact on the way with the great tribe, the *Brigantes,* in Yorkshire. The majority of the eastern settlers most probably came by sea, entering the country by means of the rivers Tweed, Forth and Tay. The characteristic structure of the western settlement is the broch, and of the eastern one, the vitrified fort. Mr Richard Feachem's map, reproduced here, illustrates their respective distributions.

Fig. 3

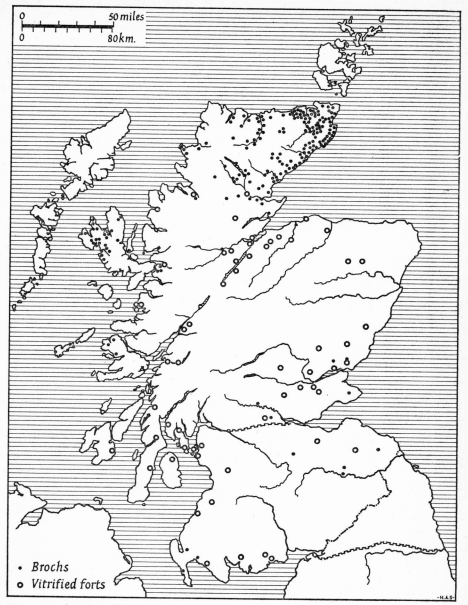

Fig. 3. Brochs and vitrified forts on the mainland. (After Feachem)

21

Plate 4

The nature of the evolution of the broch is a matter of controversy but a good case has recently been made out for its
natural development from small circular forts with hollow walls.
True brochs are tower structures often reaching as high as 60
feet and with diameters averaging about 30 feet. The people who
built the brochs were most probably of mixed origin, made up
of the native Bronze Age inhabitants as well as of the incoming
Celtic population, one strain of which, as we have seen, is to
be associated with the later phase of the British Iron Age as
manifested in *Brigantia*.

True brochs are surprisingly uniform in design, perhaps suggesting that they were built as a solution to a particular political
situation. The height of the brochs implies that the broch builders expected their opponents to be superior in numbers only and
that all that was required of the broch household in the way of
defence was to prevent the enemy from climbing in. Recently,
interesting work has been done in detecting different phases of
broch building. It has been suggested, for example, that the first
occupation of the brochs was comparatively short-lived but that
a revival of interest in the usefulness of the broch structure took
place on the northern mainland in response to the Severan punitive expeditions at the beginning of the third century AD. In
less disturbed areas it can be shown how the brochs early fell
into disuse, their sites often being re-occupied by the related
wheel-house farmers.

Plate 15

Fig. 4

A vitrified fort is normally oval or oblong in shape. The dry
stone walls were laced with timber and the intentional or ac-
cidental firing of these timbers produced temperatures capable
of fusing the stonework. The timber-lacing technique approximates to that described by Caesar as *Murus Gallicus,* but only
one Scottish fort, that at Burghead, Moray, had the correct
securing of the timbers with iron rivets, and recent opinion
holds that the Scottish examples do not derive from imperfectly
remembered Gaulish protoypes, but are part of a long-estab-

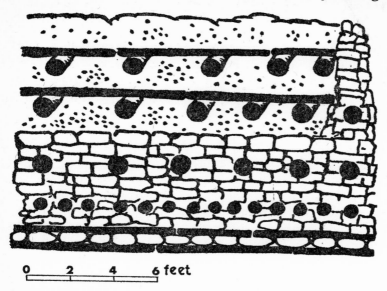

0   2   4   6 feet

Fig. 4. Elevation of the rampart at Burghead, Moray, showing timber lacing. (After Young)

lished building tradition found in structures in Wales and Northern England, which belong to the earlier phase of the British Iron Age, itself derived from continental prototypes.

Since the arrival of the broch builders in the far north coincided more or less with the arrival of the fort-builders to the south, the question naturally arises as to what kind of relationship, if any, existed between the two groups. Opinions vary on this point. Sir Lindsay Scott believed that there was no evidence of conflict between them. The boundaries between the two cultures did not fluctuate and the distributions of their artifacts were mutually exclusive. On the other hand, more recently, Mr J. R. C. Hamilton has written, 'Their mutually exclusive distribution certainly hints at hostile relations between the two people.' He would attribute the firing of many of the timber-laced forts to the broch men and sees the distribution of the forts as revealing a defended frontier system built along the edge of the broch province. He brings forward considerable archae-ological and historical evidence to support his view, including the natural antipathy of a sea-faring people to the mainland fort-dwellers.

By the time of the historical Picts of the fourth century, the broch culture was in decay. Structures relating to the broch-building tradition appeared in the fourth century in the west, but by this period brochs as such were evidently either unfash-ionable or unnecessary. What happened after one particular broch fell into disuse can be seen in the unique stratigraphic conditions pertaining at Jarlshof, Shetland, as revealed by Mr Hamilton in his comprehensive report on the excavations there.

The Jarlshof broch had a courtyard wall, and a section of this was used in the immediately post-broch phase to build a large round house within the court. This was occupied by descen-dants of the natives who had provided the labour to build the broch. In the second or early third century AD a new people arrived, probably from the north of Scotland. They introduced many changes in the economy and built their dwellings, which were wheel-houses, from stones taken from the broch tower it-self. The best preserved wheel-house at Jarlshof is a circular structure with a diameter of 24 feet. The central hearth area is surrounded by seven roofed bed recesses separated from each other by walls of masonry, the whole suggesting the wheel design implied by the name.

The wheel-house phase at Jarlshof lasted a long time, the houses remaining habitable up to the early ninth century when the Norsemen arrived on the site. During the later period of wheel-house occupation Shetland was in all likelihood part of the kingdom of the Picts.

Plate 5

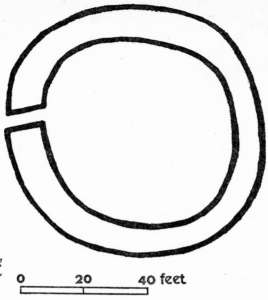

Fig. 5. Dun Geal ring fort, Glen Lyon, Perthshire. (After Watson)

0   20   40 feet

Timberlaced forts have a long history and it has been emphasized that some of them could have been built or occupied by historical Picts; the same could be said of numerous remains of premedieval fortifications in the main Pictish area. Recently, these structures have undergone systematic collection and classification by Mr Feachem. A brief indication of some of his results is given here.

Descriptions of potentially Dark Age structures repeatedly refer to the incorporation of natural features, such as rock outcrops, to augment the artificially constructed defences, and this characterizes some of the simplest of the fort types – the ringfort. These forts appear within the Pictish area, but as far as is at present known, not in any degree of concentration. Some of them at least may be the work of the Scots, who had established the kingdom of Dalriada in southwestern Pictish territory during the second half of the fifth century. In such a context the

Fig. 5

Plate 9

Perthshire examples would be of particular interest, standing as they do on passes leading from the west into the heart of Pictland.

The simple ring-fort, typologically, and in all probability chronologically, develops additional defences, sometimes contemporary with the building of the fort. A similar structure could be obtained by placing a new ring-fort within a much older defensive structure. The way in which older sites were re-used is exemplified well in the series of structures on Turin Hill, Angus. Here the ring-fort has been placed within an oval structure recalling in shape and size the vitrified-fort type, which in its turn had been partly superimposed on an Early Iron Age fort with double ramparts.

Fig. 6

The next ground plan in the series can most naturally be interpreted as the result of the desire to reproduce the advantages of these converted sites, but to place them on the rocky kind of ground preferred by the builders. In 1949 Mr R. B. K. Stevenson isolated a type of fortification falling within this class which he called the 'nuclear fort', for its plan comprised a cluster of enclosures looping out from the ring-fort-type citadel. The particular interest of the nuclear fort ground plan is that it is found

Fig. 6. Plan of the fortifications on Turin Hill, Angus. (After Christison)

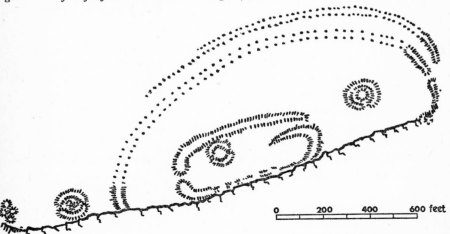

0   200   400   600 feet

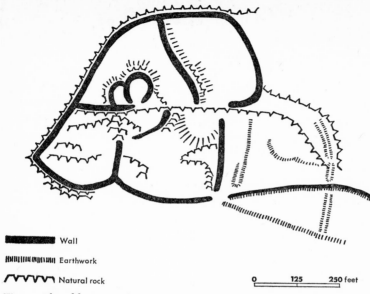

Wall

Earthwork

Natural rock

0   125   250 feet

Fig. 7.   Plan of fort at Dundurn, Perthshire. (After Christison and Feachem)

together with sites known from written sources to have been of
importance in the Dark Age period. For example, the design
of Dunadd, Argyll, is 'nuclear' and excavation there produced
finds which link the occupation of the fort firmly with the Dark
Ages. In addition, Dunadd is mentioned repeatedly in the Irish
Annals as a stronghold of the Scots of Dalriada in the seventh
and eighth centuries. Of special importance for the history of
the Picts is the recognition of the nuclear plan of the fortification on Dundurn, Perthshire. A siege *(obsessio)* of Dundurn is
recorded in the Irish *Annals* towards the end of the seventh
century and it can be fairly safely assumed that the remains at
Dundurn are those of a fortification occupied by the Picts at
this time.

Structures built as fortifications have naturally survived the
ages best but a large part of the population, at all times, must

Fig. 7

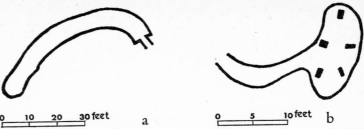

Fig. 8. Souterrain *types: a. Airlie I, Angus. b. Hatston, Orkney. c. Allt Cille*

have been housed in much humbler dwellings, probably small, roughly circular huts of stone and wattle. The structure commonly known as a *souterrain* or earth-house belongs to this category of less ambitious domestic building.

The *souterrain*, unlike the structures discussed above, has a distribution which covers the whole of the kingdom of the historical Picts. Finds suggest that the majority were built in the second and third centuries AD. They stand, therefore, much closer to the Picts than, for example, do brochs.

Fig. 8a, b, c, d

A typical *souterrain* found in southern Pictland takes the form of a spacious underground passage sometimes as long as 80 feet. It is about 8 feet wide and 6 feet high. The passage is curved and it broadens towards the end to form a terminal bulge. In the far north the *souterrain* plan looks much more like a dwelling, and finds confirm this. The shorter, more constricted passage *souterrains* of Aberdeenshire, on the other hand, may well have been used as store-rooms only. The comparatively spacious passage type in southern Pictland poses a more difficult problem, for it is too small for a dwelling but is unsuitably large for a store-room. Dr Wainwright has put forward a good case, based on structural details, for their being used primarily as cattle shelters for use in the winter months.

Plate 6

Dr Wainwright's excavation of two Angus *souterrain* sites at Ardestie and Carlungie, Angus, are of special interest. At both

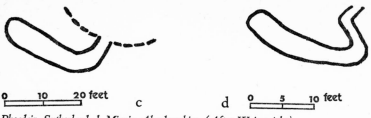

0   10   20 feet   c   d   0   5   10 feet

Pheadair, Sutherland. d. Migvie, Aberdeenshire. (After Wainwright)

of these sites the occupants of the surface structures associated with the *souterrain* deliberately demolished it and proceeded to reorganize their surface dwellings. There was no break in the occupation so that the existence of this post-*souterrain* settlement, which must belong to the period of the historical Picts, proves that the *souterrain* builders were forebears of the historical Picts.

THE PICTISH LANGUAGE

One of the most important advances in Pictish studies in recent years has been Professor Jackson's analysis of the sources for the nature of the language spoken by the Picts. Since not a single sentence in this tongue has survived on vellum, the sources for Pictish comprise brief monumental inscriptions, place-names, and occasional references in classical and Dark Age writers. Professor Jackson's conclusions, after examining this material, may be summarized as follows.

Pictish Celtic belonged to the P-Celtic, that is the Brittonic branch of the Celtic languages. It shares with Gaulish Celtic features that are not found in British Celtic. Some such differ-ence is to be expected, since the individuality of Pictish Celtic is commented upon by Dark Age writers. This Pictish Celtic, which may suitably be called Gallo-Brittonic, has left its clearest traces in certain place-names, notably those containing the

29

element *Pit-*, a type of name unknown south of the Forth-Clyde line. These place-names are distributed thickly throughout the main Pictish area from south-east Sutherland to the Forth, the districts which belong to the four great tribes in Ptolemy and where the vitrified forts discussed above are found. Professor Jackson has very tentatively suggested that the differences between Brittonic Celtic and Pictish Celtic could be a consequence of the proposed Hallstatt derivation of the vitrified fort builders, for in the south the dialect spoken by the Celts of the Hallstatt period would have been overlaid by the speech of the later La Tène Celts.

Professor Jackson envisages the Gallo-Brittonic speakers mingling with the Bronze Age natives, adopting some of their tribal names, and even to some degree their language, which was in all probability non-Indo-European. He argues that the non-Indo-European element must have been quite strong, for the incoming Celts did not swamp the natives linguistically and, moreover, appear to have adopted the latter's law of succession through the female.

In the far north and west the situation is somewhat different. Here the incoming Celts of La Tène background have left remarkably few traces of P-Celtic names. Subsequent repopulation by the Irish and Norse may account for this in part, but Professor Jackson believes that the contrast is sufficiently striking to suggest that 'the immigrants of the north-west gave up their Celtic speech almost entirely, adopting that of the Bronze Age natives who may have constituted the bulk of the population under a Celtic aristocracy'.

All this sheds a unique light on the relations between the Celtic immigrants and the native population during the last centuries BC and the first centuries of our era in both cultural zones. It will be realized, however, that while the evidence available for linguistic analysis is unlikely to undergo any great change and can stand independently, the archaeological pattern

on which the results of the analysis have been tentatively imposed, is less stable. One writer has already suggested that the
introduction of this Gallo-Brittonic Celtic to Scotland could
be associated with the growing body of archaeological evidence
suggesting contacts *circa* 500 BC between eastern Scotland and
continental Celts of the Hallstatt period of the Iron Age.

The great majority of Dark Age inscriptions in Pictland appear to have been written in the language of the older population. They are written for the most part, in the Irish Ogam
alphabet, a highly formalized system of writing in which short
incised lines are scored across a long incised line or stone edge,
the particular angle and number of short-lines signifying individual letters. The Picts presumably learned this alphabet
from the Scots of Dalriada, the variety of Ogam used suggesting
a date about the eighth century for its introduction to Pictland.
The interpretation of the reading of the inscriptions has been
the subject of much controversy, but Professor Jackson's view
of them as meaningful personal names holds the field at present.
Much of their apparent obscurity is due no doubt to their containing unfamiliar proper names, and a further basic difficulty
may be that the non-Indo-European language of the Picts was
never a written language.

Plate 24

PICTISH TRIBAL CUSTOMS

In narrating a learned legend concerning the origin of the Picts
Bede writes that 'whenever doubt arises they choose a king from
the female royal lineage rather than from the male: which custom, as is well known, has been observed among the Picts to
this day.' The legend is historically valueless but Bede's comment shows that matrilinearism was practised among the Picts
in the eighth century. His qualification, 'whenever doubt arises',
may safely be discounted, and may in fact only intend the
meaning 'whenever the throne is vacant'.

Comparison with the independent Irish *Annals* makes it quite clear that the list of Pictish kings represents a chronological consecutive succession of national rulers. In the list, no son succeeds a father, except in, at most, two cases towards the end. Brothers, on the other hand, regularly succeed one another. The succession could clearly be broken by powerful usurpers but a usurping son of a king never seems to have been able to find a following.

Since this system of succession is not found in other Celtic contexts it is highly probable that it came from the native Bronze Age culture.

Classical comment on Pictish sexual customs implies the practice of some sort of polygamy by the northern tribes. Matrilinearism may have been adopted simply as a solution to the practical problem of proving paternity, but on the other hand polygamy may have always accompanied matrilinearism, as a means of assisting adherence to a religious and legal taboo preventing the succession of a son.

It is surprising that there is no reference in Dark Age sources to the reaction of the Church to Pictish marriage customs. Sparse though the sources are, some comment might reasonably be expected in Adomnan or Bede if the behaviour of the Picts in these matters had been particularly lax. There can have been no question of the tolerance of polygamy, however controlled, among the Picts after the conversion. Matrilinearism, however, can still be made to operate in a monogamous society, the important marriages being that of a king's sister and that of his daughter.

Under a polyandrous or generally polygamous system, the identity of the father of the new king was obscured, and the fact that this convenient ignorance was no longer possible may have encouraged another practice attributed to the Picts, that of exogamy, where the marriage partner has to be found outside the tribe. There are only two certain examples of exogamy in the historical period but the neighbouring kingdom of Dalriada would have provided a convenient supply of foreign princes, and, as is often remarked, such intermarriages could have helped to undermine Pictish solidarity. There is no real evidence, however, that Pictish society was exogamic.

In addition to the sexual promiscuity of the Picts, Classical writers were struck by their habit of personal tattooing. A recent examination of this material by Dr Nora Chadwick reveals how few of these accounts are independent and how little direct knowledge lies behind any of them. Dr Chadwick suggests that there is a real possibility that the picture of the Picts tattooed with weird designs belongs simply to 'the *mirabilia* which the Romans and Alexandrians loved to record of the barbarians whom they had conquered'. This is certainly the *genre* into which the Classical tradition degenerated, an example of which can be seen in the utterly Classical but marvellously tattooed drawing of a Pict by John White, which is included among the plates.

Plate 2

Here, the Roman name, *Picti*, is itself part of the evidence, for if it is simply a Latin adjective and not a latinization of a native name, with no semantic significance, then the point of the description must be that the Picts painted themselves in some manner. There is also the older name *Priteni* to consider. This is the northern form of the name *Pritani* used of the people of south Britain in the early phase of the Iron Age. It means 'people of the designs' and presumably refers to tattooing or painting, a habit acquired perhaps from an older population. The habit might well have travelled north at the time of the refugee movements described earlier.

The evidence is not good but the combination of the Classical tradition, however encrusted with fanciful detail, together with the evidence implicit in the names *Priteni* and *Picti,* still leaves the possibility open that the northern tribes did in fact tattoo themselves as late as the fourth century AD.

TERRITORIAL DIVISIONS IN THE HISTORICAL PERIOD

We have seen that there is some evidence that the four tribes which occupy central Scotland in Ptolemy's map formed themselves into two confederacies and in the early Roman period it is quite clear that the *Caledonii* and *Maeatae* considered themselves entirely independent. It is equally clear that the Romans did all they could to foster this division. However, by the end of the third century the Picts were acting together and, moreover, in alliance with the Scots. The high water mark of this movement towards military, if not political, unity was the great raid of AD 367 when Picts, Scots, Franks and Saxons attacked Britain simultaneously. In the late fourth century AD, Ammianus Marcellinus still wrote of the Picts as comprising two peoples but by the middle of the sixth we have a truly historical king of all the Picts, Bridei, son of Maelcon.

Writing of the time of Bridei, Bede tells how St Columba preached 'to the provinces of the northern Picts', while St Ninian 'a long time before', had converted the 'southern Picts'. These words of Bede's are generally taken as evidence for the division of the Picts into two political groups, the north and the south, during the period AD 400 to 600, or even until about 735, for Bede writes in the present tense. Historians have capitalized 'southern' and 'northern' and written of kings of the Northern Picts fighting kings of the Southern Picts, and so on.

It is difficult to decide whether Bede's words bear this interpretation or whether his use of 'northern' and 'southern' is merely geographical. In its context, the conception of the Picts as comprising 'northern Picts' and 'southern Picts' allows Pictland to be converted in two stages by two pioneer saints, Ninian and Columba. This perhaps suggests that the division of the Picts has only appeared to accommodate the story of Ninian's work among the Picts, and that as soon as the story is told it is promptly forgotten. This suspicion, together with the ambiguity of Bede's terms, makes it extremely doubtful if a belief in the political independence of the north and south in the early historical period can justifiably be based on this passage in Bede alone.

The earliest text of the list of Pictish kings, which belongs to the tenth century, or earlier, records a long list of kings for the centuries before the historical period. The first king of the Picts is said to have been *Cruithne,* and his seven sons reigned after him. This is clearly an eponymous story, a *genre* much loved by the pseudo-historian. *Cruithni,* as we have seen, is the name which the Irish gave to the Picts of the historical period and it is likely that this eponymous tale was made up by an Irishman, a fact which would also account for the anomalous succession of the sons after the father. The seven sons are called *Fib, Fidach, Foltlaig, Fortrenn, Caitt, Ce,* and *Circinn,* and some of these names can be identified with Pictish districts mentioned in the Irish *Annals* and elsewhere; *Fib* is Fife; *Fortrenn* represents the Pictish district *Fortriu; Foltlaig,* sometimes *Fotla,* is the Pictish district *Athfotla,* modern Atholl; *Circinn* is the name of a Pictish district, which from later place-names we know to have been Angus; *Caitt* is Caithness; a case has been made for identifying *Ce* as Aberdeenshire, with its mountain Bennachie; the identification of *Fidach* is uncertain.

On the basis of these undoubtedly old and valuable names it is often said that the historical kingdom of the Picts was divided into seven provinces, but it has to be remembered that the only evidence on this point is this foreign writer's eponymous tale of uncertain date. He may only have known seven Pictish district names.

A twelfth-century tract known as *De Situ Albanie* attempts to develop a version of the eponymous tale of Cruithne and his sons. It tells how the land was divided in ancient times into seven parts by the seven brothers, and the divisions are described as follows:

Fig. 9

1. Angus with the Mearns
2. Atholl and Gowrie
3. Strathearn and Menteith
4. Fife with Fothreff
5. Mar and Buchan
6. Moray and Ross
7. Caithness 'to this side of the mountain'
Caithness 'beyond the mountain'

Andrew, the Bishop of Caithness, told the author of the extent of these seven kingdoms, and they are given thus:

1. Forth to the Tay
2. Tay to the Hilef (perhaps the River Isla in Angus)
3. Hilef to the Dee
4. Dee to the Spey
5. Spey to Druimalban
6. Moray and Ross
7. Argyll

It is generally thought that since the account of the seven divisions of the brothers includes Caithness, but omits Argyll, it represents a survey of the Pictish area during the period of Pictish supremacy, and that since Bishop Andrew's account omits Caithness, but includes Argyll, it represents Scotland after the union of the Picts and Scots. It should be noticed, however, that the author intended Bishop Andrew's account to represent the seven kingdoms ruled over by the sons. The tract is in fact a much more careless piece of work than writers have admitted and its evidence should not be given too much weight. The most valuable part of the *De Situ Albanie* is probably the five land boundaries given to the author of the tract by the Bishop of Caithness; it is these boundaries, if anything, with which the eponymous sons of *Cruithne* should be compared.

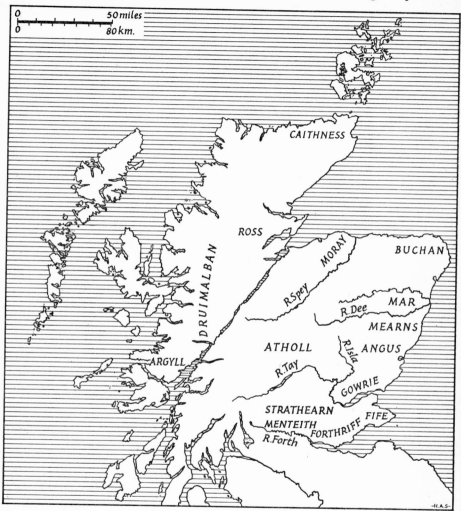

Fig. 9. Names from the De Situ Albanie

Plate 7

Plate 8

Plate 1

As early as AD 80 Agricola had made a political boundary of the Forth-Clyde line. This forward position was not maintained long, and by AD 125 the new line from Tyne to Solway was being spanned by the wall of Hadrian. Had the Hadrianic policy of recession been maintained, it is possible that a measure of unity between the tribes on either side of the Forth-Clyde line might have resulted. The middle of the second century, however, saw a second invasion of the territories north of the wall and the Agricolan line restored. Here, a new wall, the Antonine Wall, was built, again a formidable barrier but this time built of turf. The commemorative slab at Bridgeness, near Bo'ness at the eastern end of the wall, vividly portrays the relative position of Roman and native at this time.

Following the disastrous raids of the northern tribes and the subsequent punitive campaign of Severus and his sons at the beginning of the third century, the Antonine line was abandoned but the forward area to the north of the Hadrianic frontier became a protectorate. The northern frontier was at peace thereafter for nearly a hundred years and it was this peaceful period which set the seal on the extent of the historical kingdom of the Picts. The tribes to the south of the Forth-Clyde line were irrevocably committed to the Province, while the tribes to the north were equally irrevocably committed to its enemies.

From the end of the third century the Picts played a full part in the incessant raiding with which Britain was plagued on all sides. In the great raid of AD 367 the Wall was heavily damaged and in the hasty reorganization which followed the protectorate states to the north were allowed to take over their own defence while maintaining their allegiance to the Province. It is to this period therefore that the origin of the later, powerful North British kingdoms belongs. The withdrawal of the frontier troops by Magnus Maximus in AD 383 led, inevitably, to an invasion of the northern frontier. The tribes descended on the Wall and great damage was done. This time there was no rebuilding.

After this period there is very little information available for the state of affairs in the north. Contemporary panegyrists maintain that in the time of Flavius Stilicho (*c.* 395) Britain no longer had to fear Pict, Scot or Saxon. In 401, however, Stilicho withdrew his troops in order to fight against the Goths. Various usurpers took his place in Britain, the last of whom, Constantine, also went over to Gaul with the British troops.

The Britons were now left alone to deal with the increasing numbers of sea-raiders and land-plunderers. They appealed for help to the Emperor Honorius, but in his reply, written in 409, he told them bluntly that they must look after themselves.

At first the Britons seem to have managed reasonably well. The British kingdoms to the immediate south of the Forth-Clyde line must have been under considerable pressure from the Picts, but the departure of the Romans saw no expansion on their part at the expense of the British, such as one might have expected. The North British kingdoms held their own, and indeed there is some evidence that the Northern Britons of the kingdom of *Manaw Gododdin,* the northern frontier of which included the southern shores of the Firth of Forth, were able to come to the aid of the Britons further south who were in danger of being swamped by Irish intrusion in the west, probably in the mid-fifth century.

Shortly after this period the Irish kingdom of Dalriada was established in the south-west corner of Pictish territory. Scottish raiding, followed in many cases by settlement, was no doubt common on the western shores of the Pictish mainland but how and why these sporadic movements organized themselves into a fully-fledged kingdom is not known. Bede states quite clearly that Dalriada was colonized at the expense of the Picts, but he has no information on how this came about. He comments vaguely that it was achieved 'either by friendship or by the sword'. The settlement could have had its origin in the apparent alliance of the Picts and Scots as the common enemies of Roman Britain, or the Scots may simply have driven out the Pictish inhabitants. One suggestion has been that the kingdom was established with the help of the Britons of Strathclyde, and that they may indeed have initiated the settlement in order to provide a buffer between themselves and the Picts. This Roman frontier practice might well have been adopted by a kingdom which had been in prolonged contact with the Roman military.

Whatever the original terms of the settlement, by 550, when the first historical king of the Picts, Bridei, son of Maelcon, came to the throne, relations between the Scots of Ireland and Dalriada, and the Picts, were definitely hostile in a way that is never hinted at in earlier centuries.

At this same period a group of English invaders had established themselves on the rock of Bamburgh. This seemingly insignificant settlement, together with another further south, was to form the great kingdom of Northumbria which reached the height of its power in the seventh century. Bridei, king of the Picts, preoccupied with containing the Scottish settlement within narrow bounds, was probably not even aware of this new element in northern politics.

By 550 the composition of Dark Age Scotland was falling into place. The Picts controlled the country roughly to the north of the Forth-Clyde line, with the exception of the lands in the south-west held by Dalriada. This powerful kingdom of the Britons of Strathclyde lay to the south of Dalriada. On the east, the British kingdom of *Manaw Gododdin* held the southern shores of the Forth and probably extended northwards as far as the Stirlingshire plain. This kingdom was eventually swallowed up by the English probably early in the seventh century.

It was inevitable that the four peoples clustering round the Forth-Clyde line should be in perpetual conflict. All had individual backgrounds – Gaels, Britons, Picts, and Angles.

Fig. 10

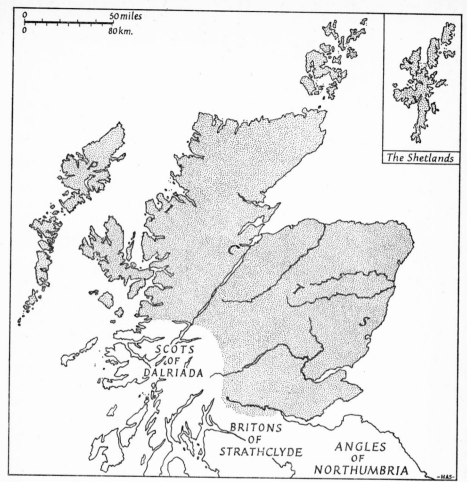

Fig. 10. *North Britain around AD 650*

There was no obvious natural alliance between any two of them and, when alliances did occur, they were temporary affairs soon forgotten. When a fifth group, the Norse, appeared in the ninth century, the whole perilous balance collapsed and the ancient kingdom of the Picts was lost in the wreckage.

CHAPTER II

The Kings of the Picts

THE DATES OF THE DEATHS of the kings and the battles they fought provide the bulk of the evidence available for the history of the Picts and even these brief notices are to be found only in foreign sources where there is no guarantee that the battles recorded represent a complete and logical series such as might be assumed in a native record. Where we know anything about a king, other than his military prowess, it is because he was concerned with an important ecclesiastical event which caught the attention of some interested foreign monastic scrip/torium. For example, the part played by Bridei, son of Maelcon, in the conversion of the Picts by St Columba is recorded by Adomnan of Iona, and the reformation of the church in Pict/land brought about by Nechton, son of Derelei, is written up by Bede as part of the work of his own abbot at Wearmouth and Jarrow. These ecclesiastical innovations by Pictish kings together with some of the less well attested developments in the church in Pictland will be discussed in a later chapter. Here we are concerned only with the military capacities of the kings and how they affected the history of the nation. In this period leadership was all/important and the emergence or untimely loss of a successful king/general could change the fortunes of a nation dramatically from one year to the next.

Of the long list of kings of the Picts in the historical period only three made any sustained impression on contemporary foreign annalists. Fortunately these three span the centuries. For the sixth century there is Bridei, son of Maelcon, for the seventh century Bridei, son of Bili, and for the eighth century Onuist, son of Uurguist – the Oengus mac Ferguso of Irish sources. Even about these three comparatively little is known. There is enough, however, to testify certainly to the normal, and on

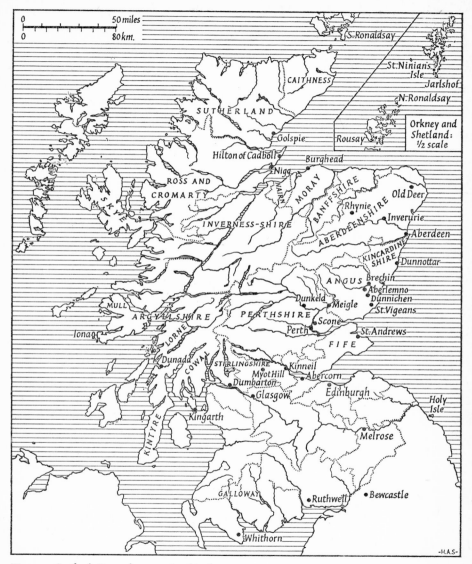

Scale:
0 — 50 miles
0 — 80 km.

S.Ronaldsay

St.Ninian's Isle
Jarlshof

N.Ronaldsay

CAITHNESS

Rousay

Orkney and Shetland: ½ scale

SUTHERLAND

Golspie

Hilton of Cadboll
Burghead

Nigg

ROSS AND CROMARTY

SKYE

NAIRN

MORAY

BANFFSHIRE

Rhynie

ABERDEENSHIRE

Old Deer

Inverurie

INVERNESS-SHIRE

Aberdeen

KINCARDINE SHIRE

Dunnottar

ANGUS

Brechin

Aberlemno

Dunkeld

Meigle

Dunnichen

St.Vigeans

MULL

ARGYLLSHIRE

PERTHSHIRE

Scone

Iona

LORNE

Perth

St.Andrews

Dunadd

COWAL

FIFE

STIRLINGSHIRE

Kinneil

Myot Hill

Abercorn

Dumbarton

Glasgow

Edinburgh

Holy Isle

KINTYRE

Kingarth

Melrose

GALLOWAY

Ruthwell

Bewcastle

Whithorn

-H.A.S-

Fig. 11. Scotland. Some places mentioned in the text

43

occasions exceptional, military prowess of the Picts with all that this implies in terms of man-power, strategy, equipment, and transport. These kings of the Picts take their place with the other great battle-kings of the Irish, Britons and Angles in what Adomnan vividly describes as 'the dreadful clashings of wars' that were fought year after year among those neighbouring peoples for the supremacy of southern Scotland in the post-Roman period.

THE REIGN OF BRIDEI, SON OF MAELCON

Post-Roman Pictish history begins with the reign of Bridei, son of Maelcon, for he is the first king in the king list to be mentioned in an independent historical source. His father's name, Maelcon, is the equivalent of Maelgwn, the king of North Wales, whose family is said to have originated in the district south of the Forth which was in British hands at this time. Maelgwn died in 547, and it is perfectly possible that this powerful Welsh king was in fact Bridei's father.

About five years after the beginning of his reign Bridei defeated the Scots of Argyll. In the same year the death of their king, Gabran, is recorded. Gabran's family had settled in Knapdale and Kintyre in the fifth century and the family play an important part throughout the history of Dalriada. It is not clear whether this 'flight of the Scots before Brude, son of Maelcon' was a decisive Pictish victory, but its appearance in the Irish *Annals* at this point reflects its importance and no fighting between the Picts and Scots is recorded for the following fifteen years.

According to Adomnan's *Life of Columba*, Columba visited Gabran's nephew and successor, Conall, son of Comgall, immediately before going to Iona for the first time. Comgall's family occupied the area east of Loch Fyne, still known by his name, Cowal. They also came to control the regions to the west of the loch up to the coast. During Columba's visit, there can be no doubt that the problem of Conall's Pictish neighbours was fully discussed. It is possible indeed that the mission to the Picts was undertaken expressly at the request of Conall at a time when Dalriada was being pressed.

The chief source of information for the conversion of the Picts by Columba is Adomnan's *Life*. Adomnan, ninth abbot of Iona, wrote the *Life* towards the end of the seventh century, nearly a hundred years after the death of Columba. For his information Adomnan was able to draw on written records and on the testimony of 'trustworthy men who knew the facts'; but Adomnan, naturally, was concerned not so much with the facts of Columba's life as with the facts of his sanctity.

The part played by Bridei himself in Adomnan's account is unfortunately almost entirely conventional. He is simply the Pagan King confronted by the Missionary Saint. The actual encounter between Bridei and Columba must have been far removed from Adomnan's picture of a wizard-saint on the one hand and a cowering baffled king on the other. It is a picture, however, which has dominated many later treatments of the subject. A typical example is the detail from a mural by the nineteenth-century artist William Hole, which is illustrated here. The burly Bridei sits utterly transfixed by the performance of the spiritual, almost ethereal, Columba. Adomnan's narrative, from the hagiographer's point of view, represents by perfectly accepted means the spiritual superiority and strength of his God-aided hero in comparison with the vulnerability of the godless pagans, but of course it tells little about the historical Bridei.

Surrounded by Christian neighbours, Bridei cannot have been unaware of the existence and general character of the Christian faith. When he heard of the arrival of Columba, and of his wish to inaugurate a mission, he must have considered carefully the advantages and disadvantages of giving Columba

Plate 3

45

leave to proceed. The advantages were largely those of status and the desirable consequence of neutralizing this particular common bond between the Irish in Britain and the Britons. On another level, he may simply have thought that the God of the Christians seemed a more powerful god than the gods of the Picts. The chief disadvantage was the release of a flood of Irish influence throughout the country.

In the end Bridei agreed to Columba's request, a step that had to be taken sooner or later. It was, however, another move in the gradual process whereby the independence of the Picts was being undermined by the Scots. The first had been when the Irish settlement had succeeded in establishing itself permanently on Pictish territory, and now the religious life of the Picts was in the control of the head of the church in Dalriada.

By far the most circumstantial fact in the passages on the Picts in Adomnan's *Life* is the location of Bridei's royal fortress near the River Ness. This fortress has not been identified, although it has been suggested by many writers that it might have been built on the site of the vitrified fort at Craig Phadrig. Adomnan does not say whether this northerly fortress was Bridei's permanent residence or whether he was simply in the district temporarily when Columba visited him. The natural assumption, however, is that Bridei was where Columba expected him to be, that is, on his permanent home ground. Bede, whose information on this point came most probably from the Picts themselves, implies that Bridei, a 'most powerful king', ruled over all the Picts, both in the north and the south. The death of a 'Cennalath, king of the Picts', is recorded in the Irish *Annals* during the reign of Bridei but he was probably a subject king who reigned jointly with Bridei for a short period.

Adomnan's *Life* does not help a great deal in determining the exact extent of the kingdom of the Picts in Bridei's time. In virtually the only incident involving him which is not entirely conventional, Bridei is said to have been in control of the

Orkneys. The 'regulus' of the Orkneys was at the Pictish court and Bridei held his hostages. The need for hostages perhaps suggests that the Orkneys had once had, and might have again, a measure of political independence.

Although incidents on several of the western isles are reported by Adomnan, in most cases there is no positive clue as to which of the islands were Irish and which Pictish. After the visit to Bridei, Columba and his followers were presumably welcome on Pictish or Irish territory. An exile from 'a noble family of the Picts' is sent to Islay for protection, which implies that this island was Irish. There are no symbols of the early type on Islay. In the *Life*, Columba visits Skye on two occasions and it is there that he meets the mysteriously styled Pictish leader of the 'cohort of Geona' whom he baptizes with the assistance of an interpreter. There are a number of symbol stones on Skye and one each on Benbecula and Pabbay to the west of the island across the sea of the Hebrides. If Bridei ruled from the Inverness area, then it is probable that he controlled Glen More and the districts to the immediate west of the Glen as far as the Hebrides. It is difficult to determine the line of the boundary between the Picts and the Irish on the west. Skene thought that it ran along Loch Leven, through Morven and thence through the island of Mull, cutting the island in two. It can be assumed that whoever controlled Mull owned Iona, so that the circumstances surrounding the donation of the island to Columba ought to help in defining the boundary between the two peoples at this time. Unfortunately, Adomnan, most surprisingly, says nothing about the donation of Iona.

THE PICTS AND AIDAN, SON OF GABRAN, KING OF DALRIADA

About 574 Conall died, and his first cousin Aidan, son of Gabran, became king of Dalriada. Aidan was an able and ambitious leader and he follows Bridei as the next substantial figure in early Scottish history. Shortly after Aidan's accession 'many allies of the sons of Gabran were killed in a battle in Kintyre'. The victors may have been the Picts but they could equally well have been the insular Irish. Six years later, the Irish *Annals* record a campaign in the Orkneys by Aidan. This certainly looks like an encroachment on Pictish territories, but if the Orkneys were on occasions hostile to Bridei it is possible, as Mrs Anderson has recently suggested, that the Dalriadic fleet was in fact acting on behalf of the Picts. Aidan is next found fighting on the southern edge of Bridei's kingdom in *Manaw Gododdin* in 582.

Two years later, Bridei died. In Adomnan's *Life* there is no account of the circumstances of his death except the unfortunately typical information that Columba's curative pebble, which Bridei kept in his treasury, could not be found. At 584 the Irish *Annals* simply record the fact of Bridei's death, but a misplaced entry at 752 gives more information. It reads, 'The battle of Asreth in the land of Circin, between Picts on both sides; and in it Brude, son of Maelchon, fell.' From this it would seem that Bridei had been having trouble controlling the southern part of his kingdom.

It is possible that the close of Bridei's reign marks the end of the importance of the north in Pictish affairs. Later kings certainly seem to have been based in the south. The growing strength of the Scottish colony, together with the increasing menace of the Angles, provides ample justification for such a change. The advance of the Irish up the west coast had been temporarily halted by Bridei, but the real danger lay in Scottish penetration through the Perthshire glens into the rich lands round the firths of Tay and Forth.

The death of Bridei brought to an end the period of peaceful coexistence between the Scots and Picts and it is generally said that thereafter Aidan subjugated a considerable part of the southern districts of the Pictish kingdom. In fact there is no good evidence for Aidan's activities in these parts. He was victorious, according to Adomnan, against a people called the *Miathi,* a name which suggests some connection with the *Maeatae* of the Roman period. Adomnan does not give a date for the battle nor does he associate the *Miathi* of this period with the Picts. He records that it was an 'unhappy victory' involving the loss of many soldiers including two of Aidan's sons, Arthur and Echoid Find. It is unlikely, therefore, that the victory led to any permanent conquest in the east.

Around 598, the death in battle of two other sons of Aidan, Bran and Domingart, is recorded in the Irish *Annals.* Adomnan says that Domingart was killed in a 'rout' in England. The 'rout' is generally identified with the Battle of Degsastan, fought according to Bede in 603, but some other sortie by the Scots into English territory may be intended. One version of the Annals, the *Annals of Tigernach,* has a note concerning the deaths of Arthur and Echoid Find corruptly inserted in amongst the notice for the death of Bran and Domingart. In the note, Arthur and Echoid are said to have died 'in the battle of Circhend'. This has led certain scholars to locate Adomnan's *Miathi* in the Pictish district of *Circinn,* roughly Kincardineshire, and thereon to base arguments of wide implication concerning the internal divisions of Pictland.

It is important to recognize the nature of the corruption in *Tigernach.* The information that Aidan was conquered presumably belongs to the battle in which Bran and Domingart were killed and which we know to have been a rout. Since the note must have been by way of additional information concerning the circumstances of the deaths of Aidan's sons, Tigernach supplies neither a date nor a result for the 'battle of Circhend'. This removes some of the difficulties involved in identifying the battle with the battle of the *Miathi,* which was a victory, and which by implication in Adomnan probably took place well before 598.

Quite apart from hypothesis concerning internal divisions, the important aspect of these matters for the course of Pictish history is the association of Aidan with *Circinn*. If, at any point, he was fighting over on the east coast of Scotland, whether victoriously or not, it implies a successful advance right through the heart of the Pictish area.

These unsatisfactory fragments of material are, however, the only evidence for Aidan's alleged Pictish conquests. Aidan will undoubtedly have attempted to extend Dalriadic influence in the east, but had there been any even temporary conquest of the southern district of Pictland, then one would expect, even from the sparse sources available for this period, at least one unequivocal record of a Dalriadic victory over the Picts, instead of merely the garbled and probably late reference to a battle in *Circinn*.

A much clearer statement of Aidan's southern ambitions is given by Bede. In a highly coloured passage at the end of the first book of the *Ecclesiastical History* Bede tells how Aethelfrith, king of Northumbria, had conquered more British territory than any other English king – exterminating the British as he went and putting English in their place. Aidan, concerned at his advance, and acting perhaps on behalf of the British of Strathclyde as well as for himself, marched against Aethelfrith with a huge army which was subsequently almost completely wiped out at a battle fought at *Degsastan* in 603. The place, which was celebrated in Bede's time because of the battle, has yet to be identified. Looking back from 731 Bede comments, 'From that time, no king of the Scots dared to make war on the English to this day.'

From the point of view of the Picts the battle of *Degsastan* meant a change in the political situation. The check to the hopes of the Scots of competing with the English in the south increased the pressure of eastward Dalriadic expansion, and the repulse of the Scots led to the advance of the English frontier on the east, to the Forth. The Picts had now a new neighbour on the south, one at least as ambitious as their Scottish neighbours on the west.

THE PICTS AND NORTHUMBRIA

Information on Pictish affairs for the first half of the seventh century is virtually non-existent. All that survives is the names of the kings and their reign lengths in the king lists, confirmed with a fair degree of consistency by the *obit* entries in the Irish *Annals*. There is no evidence, therefore, for the nature of Dal-riadic-Pictish relations during this period. Domnall Brecc, grandson of Aidan, who reigned probably from about 630 to 643, had the reputation of being a powerful and effective leader. Some of Domnall's energies were taken up with consolidating his own position in Dalriada, and he also fought several important battles in Ireland. It seems likely, however, that he would have made some attempt at enlarging his kingdom at the expense of the Picts. It is possible that the battle of *Glend Mairison,* fought about 640, 'in which the people of Domnall Brecc fled', may have taken place in the Pictish district of Glen Moriston in Inverness-shire, but the identification of the name is uncertain. Domnall Brecc was killed in a battle fought in Strathcarron by the king of the Britons of Strathclyde. At this period, therefore, whatever their relations earlier, the Scots and the Britons were enemies, a highly satisfactory situation for the Picts.

It was from Northumbria, however, that the Picts received a severe blow in the seventh century, losing outright a considerable portion of the southern part of the kingdom for nearly thirty years.

Understandably, there is no information whatsoever in the Irish sources about how this came about. For the thread of the relationship between the Picts and Northumbria virtually the sole informant is Bede, and unless otherwise stated all the information which follows is based on Bede's *Ecclesiastical History*.

In 617, when Edwin of Deira took over the kingship of Northumbria, the sons of Aethelfrith of Bernicia were exiled. Some of them went to Ireland and some to the Picts. The number of Northumbrian exiles in Pictland cannot have been very great, but they were important, and their presence cannot have been uninfluential. One of Aethelfrith's sons, Eanfrith, married a Pictish princess and their son was king of the Picts from 653 to 657. In Pictland the sons of Aethelfrith and their companions clearly felt themselves quite out of the reach of Edwin and it can be assumed that Edwin had no power over the Picts.

In 632 Edwin was killed by Cadwallon, king of Gwynedd in North Wales, aided by Penda of Mercia, an alliance which caused the Northumbrians much trouble. For a matter of months Eanfrith ruled Bernicia, the northern kingdom of Northumbria, but the interesting consequences of a king of Northumbria with a son who was a potential heir to the Pictish throne did not materialize, for Eanfrith was murdered when he went to Cadwallon to arrange a peace.

In 633 Oswald restored the fortunes of Northumbria by killing Cadwallon and reuniting the kingdoms of Deira and Bernicia. The death of their leader put an end to the effective challenge of the Britons to the Northumbrian encroachment westwards. Oswald's victory may have brought him, indirectly, some measure of control over parts of British territory but it is probable that Bede exaggerates when in one place he claims that Oswald, the Saintly King, brought under his dominion the Britons, the Picts and the Scots. In another, more prosaic, passage Bede states quite clearly that Oswald's kingdom was of the same extent as Edwin's and that it was Oswiu, his brother, who first 'subdued and made tributary' the Picts and the Scots.

Bede does not give a particular date for Oswiu's conquest but he seems to imply that it was three years after his great victory of 655. At 654 the Irish *Annals* record a victory by Talorcan, son of Eanfrith and nephew of Oswiu, over the men of Dalriada, but subsequent to this there is no record of fighting between the Picts and Scots until after they had thrown off the Northumbrians.

The terms on which the Northumbrian domination came to an end in 685 show that while part of the Pictish kingdom was actually occupied by the Northumbrians, the Scots and the Britons merely lost their 'liberty'. Nennius, or his source, interprets this loss of liberty as involving the payment of tribute money. It may also have included army service—perhaps helping to police the Pictish territory held by the Northumbrians.

It is nowhere stated how much of the Pictish kingdom was occupied. Later, Abercorn, on the south side of the Firth of Forth, was chosen for the seat of the bishopric of, in Bede's words, 'the province of the Picts which at that time was subject to the English'. On the basis of this choice, opinion favours Fife, on the opposite shore, as the occupied province. Bede also writes, however, that Oswiu 'subdued the greater part of the Picts', and it is perfectly possible that the whole of Pictland south of the Mounth was in Northumbrian hands. The occupation lasted nearly thirty years. There is no hint in any of the sources whether or not the Picts regarded this as a time of oppression. The part of Pictland which remained free was, it would appear, ruled by a certain Gartnait, of whom nothing is known except that he died in 663 and was succeeded by his brother Drest.

For the years following, the Irish *Annals* record a series of events which appear to reflect some kind of civil struggle among the independent Picts. The difficulty about using this material is that it is uncertain whether all or even some of the events belong to a logical sequence, or whether they are entirely unconnected. One is able to weave them into a hypothetical narrative, but the result is of negligible historical value. Drest was deposed in 672 and this may be connected in some way with an incident recorded in the eighthcentury *Life of St Wilfred* attributed to Eddius Stephanus. According to the *Life,* in Ecgfrith's early years, just before his queen, Aethilthryth, took the veil in 672, the 'populi bestiales Pictorum', eager to put an end to the Northumbrian occupation, gathered together 'innumerable tribes from the north' and staged a revolt. Ecgfrith quelled this promptly and, it appears, ruthlessly, for it is reported that he made a bridge of Pictish corpses over two rivers, so that his army was able to pass over dryshod and massacre the remainder of the Pictish army.

In spite of the somewhat sensational tone of the account in the *Life* there seems no reason to doubt that the revolt occurred. The writer does not record why it occurred at that particular time nor who led it. There are several possible answers to these questions, but all are equally undemonstrable. Oswiu had died in 670 and a certain amount of administrative readjustment in the north when his son Ecgfrith succeeded may have given the Picts their chance. It is possible also that Ecgfrith had moved men from Pictland to help with his successful expedition to recover the province of Lindsey from Mercia. The Lindsey campaign, however, cannot be dated more closely than between the years 671 and 675.

From the account in the *Life* it would appear that the revolt was organized not from within the occupied territory but by free Pictland to the north. This suggests that in the north there was a native leader of daring and initiative, capable of commanding wide authority. Drest, as we have seen, was deposed in 672 after a reign of nine years. This could have been a consequence of the disastrous failure of the revolt or else a preliminary clearance of an ineffective leader prior to action. In the latter case the leader might have been Bridei, son of Bili, Drest's suc cessor, and the king who in the end did succeed in overthrow/ing the Northumbrians.

Bridei, the son of Bili, is the first Pictish king after Bridei, son of Maelcon, whose career caught the attention of foreign chroniclers. Like his predecessor he seems to have come of royal British stock; Bili in all probability being the Beli, son of Neithon, who was king of the Britons of Strathclyde. A note in the Bernician royal genealogies incorporated in the *Historia Brittonum* describes Bridei as the cousin of Ecgfrith, so that Bridei's mother must have been a daughter of Eanfrith, son of Aethelfrith, whose son Talorcan was king of the Picts.

As we have seen, a national disaster marked the beginning of Bridei's career as king. For the next years it is impossible to tell which of the apparently Pictish events recorded in the Irish *An/nals* are to be claimed as referring to his exploits. Skene claimed them all, and so provided a suitable background for Bridei's triumph in 685. Skene may be right, but only one of the events in the *Annals* actually has Bridei's name associated with it; a destruction of the Orkneys in 682. This brief entry is interesting in that it shows Bridei in command of a fleet and exerting his power in the far north just prior to the period when he gained full control of the south. For the year before, a siege of Dunnot/tar is recorded. The entry is important both as one of the very few references to Pictish affairs in the north/east of Scotland and as a testimony to the presence of a Dark Age fortification on Dunnottar Rock. The besieger could have been Bridei making a show of authority on his way to the Northern Isles, but this can only be a guess. A siege of *Dunbaitte* is interpreted by Skene as a reference to Bridei's activities in Dunbeath, Caithness, but this again is mere guesswork. In 683 the *Annals* record a siege of Dunadd, in Dalriada, and of Dundurn in Pictland. The first probably resulted from an internal Dalriadic dispute, the second may have been a border skirmish; neither of which had any special bearing on the career of Bridei.

Plate 13

If Bridei's early career can only be guessed at, there is no doubt at all about the nature of his greatest achievement, the victory whereby he pushed the Northumbrian frontier back permanently to the south side of the Firth of Forth. This battle is the best documented event in the history of the Picts. It received the attention of English, Irish and British writers. Their information is, moreover, quite independent, and there seems no doubt that the victory was regarded as of particular significance and importance by all the peoples of North Britain.

Bede tells how in 684, Ecgfrith, against the advice of friends, sent one, Berct, on an expedition against the Irish, whom Bede describes as 'that harmless nation which had always been most friendly to the English'. Berct carried out his commission ruthlessly, not even sparing the churches and monasteries, and brought back prisoners to Northumbria.

The next year, evidently quite undaunted by the curses of the outraged Irish clerics, and again against all advice, particularly this time from Cuthbert, Ecgfrith personally set off to the north with his army to ravage the Picts. He crossed the Forth, it seems without resistance, and then the Tay, but once in Angus he came upon the Pictish army. On sight of the Northumbrians the Picts turned and fled, and Ecgfrith, used now to carrying all before him, pursued them. But it was a trap. Ecgfrith, in Bede's words, was 'drawn into the straits of inaccessible mountains' and at what was presumably a prearranged spot the Picts turned and, joined by reinforcements, proceeded to massacre the Northumbrian army. Ecgfrith himself was slain although his bodyguard stood to the last around him. Cuthbert, touring the Roman ruins at Carlisle where he was waiting with Queen Eormenburg for news of the northern campaign, had a horrifying vision of this disastrous event, which took place on Saturday 20th May, 685.

In the Irish *Annals* the battle is called 'Bellum duin Nechtain' a name which was recognized in the nineteenth century as representing Dunnichen, the name of a small village near Forfar in Angus. At that time there were substantial remains of a fortress on the south side of the Hill of Dunnichen and, although quarrying has much reduced their scale, what is left is considered to be consistent with a Pictish settlement of the seventh century. This fortification or settlement is therefore in all probability the 'dun' of the *Annals*.

Bede does not mention any place-name in connection with the battle but it appears in later English sources as the 'battle of Nechtan's Mere' and this may well have been the name used by the Northumbrians to identify the battle. In the note in the *Historia Brittonum* telling of Bridei's relationship to Ecgfrith it is called *Gueith Lin Garan,* which has been translated as 'the battle of the Pool of the Herons'. The note came most probably from a written Strathclyde source, but since the name form given to Bridei approximates to the Pictish spelling it is possible that in *Lin Garan* the Pictish name has also been preserved. The 'mere' or 'pool' mentioned in the sources can be identified with what used to be known as the Mire of Dunnichen, a swampy lake to the east of the village. The Mire was artificially drained in the nineteenth century but a detailed land survey and an air photograph have revealed its location and extent. The actual site of the battle can therefore be located as somewhere in the comparatively limited area between the Hill to the north of the modern village and the Mire to the east.

After the battle many of the Northumbrians in Pictland were killed or enslaved, though some managed to escape. By some means Ecgfrith's body was got to Iona. Trumwine, who was Bishop of the Picts, withdrew with his monks from Abercorn. After having placed his monks in other houses, he retired with a small group of friends to Whitby. A similar exodus of nuns who had fled from their northern convent through fear of 'the barbarian army' is described in Bede's prose *Life of St Cuthbert*. The Picts recovered all the territory which had been held by the Northumbrians, and the tribute required from the Scots and Britons ceased to be exacted.

The Northumbrians never managed to reclaim the ground they had held north of the Forth for nearly thirty years. Indeed there is no evidence that they ever made any serious attempt to do so. Ecgfrith's successor, Aldfrith, maintained the northern boundary at the Forth but the southern frontier of the kingdom had to be strongly defended against the growing power of Mer' cia, and to reconquer and reoccupy the Pictish province, would have overstrained their resources.

The immediate clearance of Northumbrians from Pictish territory effected by the victory of 685 must be explained as the result of a period of military disorganization following the death of the king and the rout of the Northumbrian army. As Ecg' frith proceeded north to Angus he had no doubt attracted to his army such established forces as there were in the Northum' brian districts of Pictland, so that the victory may have dis' posed in one stroke of the invading and standing army.

The least understandable feature of the Battle of Nechtan's Mere, as it is most commonly called, is why it should have oc' curred at all. It is unsatisfactory to assume that this great liberat' ing victory happened as it were by accident, the result of an aggressive whim of Ecgfrith. To avoid this, writers have sug' gested that in 684 there may have been the beginnings of a Celtic plot to overthrow the Northumbrians – the insular Irish promis' ing to help. Ecgfrith's actions in 684 and 685 can then be inter' preted as the timely forestalling of a major rebellion. Against this view, however, stands Bede's account, which goes out of its way to emphasize the aggressive nature of both Ecgfrith's campaigns. We are left, therefore, with a victory which won Bridei, son of Bili, a place in history, which gave the Picts im' mediate political prestige such as they had never had before, and which assured them 150 years of supremacy north of the Forth, but which owed nothing to Pictish initiative.

There remains the possibility that Bede was uninformed. Ecgfrith may have had an appreciation of what was happening in the north which was outside the scope of clerics such as Cuthbert and Bede, and Ecgfrith's death would tend to reinforce the view that his cause had been unjust. Increasing Pictish guerilla warfare on the borders of the occupied province together with reports of the military prowess of the king of the free Picts may well have suggested to Ecgfrith that the time had come to act quickly. The fact that he led the campaign himself is perhaps a measure of the seriousness with which he viewed the situation.

Bridei reigned over reunited Pictland for eight years after his great victory. There is no evidence available as to how he spent these years. In the *Life of Columba* Adomnan notes that to add to their troubles the Northumbrians in 686 were being seriously troubled by the plague which was then affecting all Europe. The Picts and Scots alone had escaped it, the result, Adomnan believed, of the veneration of Columba by these nations. Bridei's last years, therefore, would seem to have been peaceful ones. He died in 693 and in the Irish annal recording his death he is given the title of 'king of Fortriu', an indication that his administration after 685 must have been centred on the south.

Bridei's successor was a certain Taran who was deposed after four years by Bridei, the son of Derelei. This Bridei may have been the grandson of Bridei, son of Bili, but the only evidence for this relationship is a fragment of obscure Irish verse.

Right at the beginning of his reign a battle is recorded between the Picts and the Northumbrians, the first for thirteen years. It seems to have been a Pictish victory, for the Northumbrian leader was killed. There are a few very brief notices in the Irish *Annals* about conflicts in the west of Scotland during Bridei's reign but they are probably to be interpreted as incidents in the numerous civil wars which dominate Dalriadic history of this period.

THE REIGN OF NECHTON, SON OF DERELEI AND
THE RISE OF OENGUS, SON OF FERGUS

Bridei died in 706 and was succeeded by his brother Nechton. Nechton, son of Derelei, is an important figure in Pictish history for he was responsible for changing the Easter observance in the Pictish church from the Celtic to the Roman usage. In the early years of his reign the Northumbrians and the Picts were again in conflict but this time the Picts were defeated. Nechton may have decided to bring to an end these profitless border skirmishes and to make an ally of Northumbria. With adroit diplomacy he brought about both political and ecclesiastical changes by an approach to the Northumbrian Church for guidance in the matter of the Easter question. The good relations thus achieved between the Picts and the Northumbrians lasted and were formally reaffirmed by Nechton's successor.

There now follows what is certainly the most interesting period of Pictish history, for the reason that at last there is a little more information available in the sources. This, in itself, of course, reflects the important nature of the events which took place. It is the period when the Picts produced their greatest military leader, Oengus, the son of Fergus — to use the Irish form of his name which in Pictish reads, Onuist, son of Uurguist. Oengus deserves to be remembered. Had his successors been able to consolidate his achievements, then modern north Britain would certainly now have been called after the Picts instead of after the Scots. Oengus won his way to the throne of Pictland in a dramatic succession of victories over a two-year period which held the interest of the Irish annalists. He showed himself far and away the ablest of four contestants for the throne, and after he was firmly established there he turned his energies to the conquest of the neighbouring kingdoms.

The first sign of civil discord in Nechton's reign comes as

early as 713 when the Irish *Annals* report that his brother Ciniod had been murdered by the king of the district of Atholl. Nechton reacted immediately by imprisoning the murderer, and this prompt reprisal seems to have put a stop to any further trouble for ten years. In 724 the *Annals* record that Nechton had entered a monastery and that Drust had succeeded him. It may be that Nechton retired voluntarily, but the following year the son of the new Pictish king was imprisoned and the year after, Nechton himself was captured, so that there seems little doubt that he was being pressed from the start. Drust's kingship was short-lived, for in 726 he was 'cast from the kingdom of the Picts, and Alpin reigned in his stead'.

The contestants in what can be called the Pictish wars of succession were as follows: Nechton, who had a long reign behind him and whose constitutional right to the throne was presumably unassailable; Drust, who had already successfully challenged Nechton's position, presumably by a show of strength; a certain Alpin who had deposed Drust but of whose earlier career nothing is known; and lastly Oengus, the ultimate victor, whose origins are equally obscure. They were all Picts, for the battles in which they engaged are described by the Irish annalists as taking place 'among the Picts themselves'. They were all presumably leaders of various districts in Pictland, men of substance, who could command a following.

Four battles were fought, before an established king of the Picts emerged. The first encounter took place some time in 728, the last on 12th August, 729. The former is called in the Irish *Annals* the *Cath Monaigh Craebi,* which has been interpreted as being Moncrieff Hill, south of Perth. This name, like all the others connected with the contest, has yet to be identified with certainty. Up to this point the contenders for the Pictish throne were, as we have seen, Nechton, the reigning king, and a certain Drust. This first battle in the series brings to the fore the other protagonists, Oengus and Alpin. The result was a clear victory for Oengus. Many on Alpin's side were slain, including his son. Oengus, cleverly, left Nechton to finish off Alpin. That same year Nechton and Alpin fought 'a pitiful battle' at what is called *Caislen Credi*. Alpin lost all his territories and all his men, and this is the last we hear of him. This victory, even though it was over an opponent already much weakened by Oengus, apparently gave Nechton sufficient credit for him to reassume the title of 'king of the Picts'.

The year 729 saw the inevitable encounter of Nechton with Oengus. The battle took place, it is reported, at *Monith Carno* near Lake *Loogdae*. Oengus was again completely victorious. The final contest called *Cath Droma Deirg Blathuug*, was fought between Drust and Oengus. Drust was killed, and Oengus, now styled 'king of the Picts', was firmly established on a hard‑won throne.

These civil battles were obviously something more than skir‑mishes between petty chieftains, otherwise they would not have been reported in the Irish *Annals* at such length. There is even a possibility that later redactors of the two major surviving col‑lections of annals, the *Annals of Tigernach* and the *Annals of Ul‑ster* have independently paraphrased even longer versions of the entries that are to be found in the original text of the *Annals*.

OENGUS AND DALRIADA

Oengus's ambitions soon led him beyond Pictland. At this stage it was evidently not his intention to attempt a southern expansion of his kingdom for, according to Bede, a peace treaty between the Picts and the Northumbrians was being observed in 731. Dalriada was the obvious target and the first clash came in 731 when Oengus's son, Brude, put to flight a Dalriadic leader. Two years later, Dungal, the son of Selbach, of the district of Lorn in Dalriada, captured Brude while he was in sanctuary on Tory Island. During this year Eochaid, the son of Eochaid, the king of Dalriada, had died and the kingdom seems to have been divided between Dungal and his cousin Muiredach, son of Ainfcellach. Eochaid's kingship of the *Dalaraide* of northern Ireland passed to Indrechtach. Oengus's task was therefore to eliminate these Irish cousins and their potential ally in Ireland.

Oengus soon took revenge on Dungal for the latter's treatment of his son, Brude. In 734 he destroyed a Dalriadic stronghold, *Dun Leithfinn,* and wounded Dungal who, in the words of the *Annals,* 'fled from the power of Oengus into Ireland'. During the campaign of 734 the king of Atholl's son was captured near Dunolly, the important Dalriadic citadel, which shows that the Picts had by now penetrated to the western seaboard. One curious incident which took place at this time was the handing-over of his brother to the Picts, by Talorc, son of Congus. It may have been that the brother was intended as a hostage but it reads as an unpleasant episode in a family feud. Certainly the Picts did not hesitate to put the brother to death, in their traditional manner, by drowning.

Oengus's campaign of 736 proved much more devastating. The *Annals* state that in this year he laid waste the districts of Dalriada. He captured the highly important fortification at Dunadd and another called *Creic.* Dungal, who had returned from Ireland, was captured, and so was his brother Feradach. A set-back at this point came with the death of Oengus's son, Brude, who had been a useful fighter. Oengus's personal achievements were followed up, however, by his brother, who in a district called *Calathross,* which has yet to be identified, led the Picts to victory against Dungal's cousin, Muiredach.

Then, for three years there appears to have been a lull in the fighting. Oengus's name next appears in the *Annals* as ordering the king of Atholl to be drowned. The steadfast allegiance of the leader of this frontier district must have been of first importance to Oengus and this order may well have been a firm riposte to some treasonable activity between the king and his Dalriadic neighbours.

In 741 Oengus confronted the remaining leader of Eochaid's divided kingdom. In two battles, which may have been fought in Ireland, Oengus defeated and killed Indrechtach of *Dalaraide*. The situation after ten years of fighting is neatly summed up by the annalist: 'The overthrow of Dalriada by Oengus, the son of Fergus.'

OENGUS AND THE BRITONS OF STRATHCLYDE

Oengus, as might be anticipated, now turned to the conquest of the British kingdom of Strathclyde. For the lasting good of the Picts he would have done much better to consolidate his position in Dalriada. The northern Britons were a strong and united people, unlike Dalriada which had been much weakened by internal dissension. Moreover, there was the complicating factor of Northumbria, whose interest was bound to be aroused by any attempt on the part of the Picts to annex territory belonging to their western neighbour.

For this new and last phase of Oengus's career the sources are naturally no longer Irish. Northumbria now had its eye on Oengus and what follows is from Northumbrian sources.

The Picts and the Northumbrians were at peace when Bede was finishing his *Ecclesiastical History* in 731. This peace had been broken at least as early as 740, when the king of Northumbria, Eadberct, is recorded as fighting with his army against the Picts. It is unlikely that Oengus had made any aggressive move towards Northumbria at this crucial point in his Dalriadic campaign. It is much more probable that Eadberct had taken the chance of Oengus's absence from Pictland to make a sortie on south Pictland. As it turned out, Aethelbald of Mercia took advantage of Eadberct's absence from his kingdom and laid waste part of Northumbria.

In 744 the first battle between the Picts and the Britons is recorded. The result is not given, so it may have been indecisive.

At 750 in the continuation of Bede's chronological recapitulation of his *History* there is a curious reference to Cuthred of Wessex 'rising against' Oengus and Aethelbald. The language seems to imply that there had been an alliance between these three kings. In 743 Aethelbald and Cuthred had fought against the Welsh, so the three had a common antipathy to the Britons. The evidence suggests that after his success in Dalriada Oengus was willing to attach himself to any king who could help him to get a foothold in Strathclyde.

In the same year, and perhaps as a result of the collapse of the alliance, the Picts, led by Oengus's brother Talorcan, were severely defeated by the Britons. This was the first major defeat of Oengus's career. Talorcan was killed in the battle, so Oengus lost not only a substantial portion of his army but the support of a brother who had proved himself a most able general. The defeat of 750 was clearly a grave set-back. The Irish *Annals* record for that year 'the ebbing of the sovereignty of Oengus'. This presumably reflects simply the annalist's surprise that luck was departing from the hitherto invincible Oengus, rather than implying any real interruption of his kingship, as is sometimes suggested.

In 756 Oengus re-allied himself with Northumbria, and he and Eadberct marched against the Strathclyde capital, the fortress of Dumbarton rock. At first they seem to have been successful, forcing the Britons to come to terms on 1st August. Ten days later, however, nearly the whole allied army was wiped out.

If the sudden silence of all the sources is to be taken as significant, this disaster was Oengus's last battle. He had achieved nothing whatsoever in his attempt on Strathclyde, whether supported or unsupported. There is no reason to suppose, however, that he did not maintain his position in Dalriada until his death five years later in 761. In the Irish *Annals* his death is recorded without comment. In the continuation of Bede his epitaph is entirely frank; 'Oengus the king of the Picts died – a tyrannical murderer who from the beginning to the end of his reign persisted in the performance of bloody crime'.

CHAPTER III

The Church and the Picts

THE TRIBES who eventually came together to form the Pictish nation would almost certainly have practised some form of idolatrous pagan religion, the rites and *personae* varying from group to group. The Celtic element in the population we can imagine as embracing at least some aspects of the Celtic pantheon known from the Gauls and other Celtic peoples. If, however, as has been suggested, there was a substantial derivation of the population from the original non-Celtic Bronze Age natives, then the nature of Pictish primitive religion becomes much more difficult to pin down.

Failing the discovery or recognition of datable cult objects (and some headway is beginning to be made in this field), folklore can be a fruitful source of clues to the general nature of the pagan beliefs of a people. No Pictish folklore has survived but scholars have suggested that certain episodes in Irish folk tales have a Pictish background and in time sufficient material to be useful in this connection may accumulate.

The abundant representational art of the Picts is another place where Pictish pagan traces may be preserved. The frontal female rider on a cross slab in Ross-shire is often compared with Gaulish representations of *Epona*, but if the sculptor had this iconography in mind, there is no way of telling whether he was inspired directly by some abandoned native cult or indirectly through some foreign model of the type which provided Pictish sculptors with many essentially learned motifs. Some of the obscure figure scenes on the stones might, however, very well represent well-known incidents in Pictish folklore which in turn might preserve echoes of pagan practices.

The earlier class of sculptures bearing only symbols brings us nearer in time to the pagan period, and putting aside all other considerations there is no doubt that the Pictish symbols fit most naturally into the context of some kind of system of pagan concepts. But no proof of such a connection is yet forthcoming.

Adomnan's *Life of Columba* provides a generalized picture of Pictish heathen practices. A caste of magi, the chief of which is an intimate of the king, worship and 'magnify their gods'. The nature of the Pictish gods is not directly stated but they seem to be deities concerned with human destiny and not to be simply vague forces. It must be said, however, that Adomnan's highly conventional treatment of the pagan opposition weakens the value of the *Life* as evidence for the early religious history of the Picts.

The nature of Pictish paganism, or paganisms, is therefore virtually unknown. The probability is that in this matter the Picts were highly individual. In that event the attributes of their old beliefs would not mingle well with the early religion of their neighbours or assimilate easily with the new Christian cult patterns, facts which might contribute to their early disappearance after the conversion.

NINIAN

Of the many controversial subjects connected with Pictish studies the part played by St Ninian in the conversion of the Picts has been one of the most acrimonious. Some scholars have gone so far as to deny that there is any good evidence for a mission by Ninian to the Picts north of the Forth-Clyde line at all. Others believe that Ninian conducted an extensive mission at least as far north as the line of the River Dee, leaving behind numerous foundations. The controversy is not helped by the general vagueness which surrounds the life and career of Ninian himself.

Much is at stake in the debate. If it can be demonstrated that Ninian conducted an effective mission to the Picts, then to him belongs the prestige due to a pioneer saint and Columba's efforts more than a hundred years later are correspondingly diminished. To some native scholars Columba stands for Irish influence and Celtic schism whereas Ninian, though a Briton, is at least not Irish, and represents conformity with Rome. Happily the cruder aspects of the nationalist motive in studies of Ninian are now in abeyance. The present concern is with the minute examination of the late written source material to detect traces of early authentic details. Previously this late material was either rejected or accepted wholesale according to the judgement of the individual scholar. These close studies are full of interest and value but the type of results which they produce is not helpful for a general study. In the following brief account attention will be drawn only to the broader aspects of the problem of Ninian's place in the history of the Church in Pictland.

Several years ago a striking archaeological discovery was claimed at Whithorn, namely, the remains of what is considered to be the church originally founded there by Ninian. The outer face of the building was covered with cream-coloured mortar and it was suggested that this was a dramatic proof that the building is in fact *Candida Casa* itself, the 'White House', which according to Bede was the popular name for Ninian's church. If the identification is accepted, then the excavation sets Ninian's lifetime in the second quarter of the fifth century.

Plate 11

It has recently been suggested, however, that the word *casa* does not aptly describe the remains of this early church. *Casa*, it seems, carries with it a definite connotation of a very humble dwelling – something in the nature of a hut. The stone building with the white-daubed walls might therefore be the work of a close successor of Ninian – a visible expression in permanent materials of the humble 'unsullied' dwelling of the saint when he first came to Whithorn. In that event Ninian's working lifetime would belong somewhat earlier in the century.

There is only one piece of evidence, apart from the material bearing directly on Ninian, for Christianity among the Picts at this period. About the middle of the fifth century St Patrick of Ireland wrote a letter, the text of which still survives, to the soldiers of Coroticus, a king of the Britons of Strathclyde. In the letter Patrick reviles the soldiers for their part in the massacre of a congregation of Christians during a raid in Ireland. Associated with them in this disreputable incident were 'the most unworthy, most evil, and apostate Picts'. The implication of this unequivocal description is that some time earlier in the century these particular Picts had been Christian, a circumstance which supports the earlier dating of Ninian.

The most important evidence both for the life of Ninian and for his mission to the Picts is a passage in Bede's *Ecclesiastical History*. In a chapter, chiefly concerned with the sixth-century mission of St Columba to the Picts, he records how, according to tradition, the southern Picts had been converted 'long ago' by Nynia, 'bishop and holy man of the nation of the Britons, who had been regularly instructed at Rome'.

Bede is most likely to have got his information from Pecthelm, the first bishop of the Anglian bishopric at Whithorn, founded just before Bede completed his *History*. Pecthelm's source most probably was a Celtic *Life of St Ninian* now lost. It is impossible to tell whether the claim that Ninian had converted the Picts was in this lost *Life,* but it is highly unlikely that the Northumbrians would have gone to the trouble to invent a claim concerning a mission to the Picts.

It would seem that Bede himself knew nothing of a Ninianic Church in Pictland, either past or present. To judge by the *History* as a whole, Bede certainly seems to have been under the impression that the Church in Pictland was entirely Columban. The only reference to Ninian is this one passage which is awkwardly inserted into an account of Columba's mission. There is something artificial in the way in which the two missionaries are assigned their separate districts, the south and the north, and the Picts converted in separate stages. No other source implies that Columba's influence was limited to the north and it is therefore perfectly possible that the Whithorn claim also covered the entire territory of the Picts.

There is no good evidence for an active flourishing Ninianic Church existing side by side with the Columban one in Pict-land at any period. The *Life of St Ninian* written in the twelfth century, where one would expect to find any floating traditions, has nothing whatsoever to add to Bede on the topic of Ninian's Pictish mission. A chapter is devoted to the mission but it is patently an attempt to say something about nothing.

There are many dedications to St Ninian in the parts of Scotland which were Pictish, but the virtually insurmountable difficulty of proving an early origin for the individual dedications renders them of little use. The remarkable find of a hoard of Plates 19–23, 25 Dark Age metalwork on St Ninian's Isle, Shetland, suggests that the pre-Norse church on the island may have been de-dicated to St Ninian in the eighth century but it has yet to be demonstrated that the dedication belongs to this period and not to the later church-history of the island. The majority of the dedications to St Ninian almost certainly belong to the period of the revival of the Ninianic cult in the twelfth century and not to the period of the Pictish supremacy.

It has been suggested that a surviving Ninianic Church formed the Roman faction which brought about the break with the Columban Church in the early eighth century. More prob-ably the Roman faction in the Church at this time had its origins in the Northumbrian occupation of Pictland and the consequent influence of Wilfred, and later Bishop Trumwine, on the Pictish churches in the occupied area.

Clear traces of Ninian's activities among the Picts are, there-fore, not to be found. We are left, however, with the high prob-ability that the first Anglican bishop of Whithorn told Bede that Ninian had converted Picts, and that his information came from an early Celtic *Life* of the Saint now lost. One considerable advance in the whole problem has been the firm laying of the ghosts of the so-called Galloway Picts who are now generally taken to have been a medieval myth. At least we now know that the Picts involved are the Picts north of the Forth-Clyde line. It would seem to be that Ninian did work among the Picts but that his results were not lasting, and such foundations as survived rapidly fused with the Columban Church, forgetting and being forgotten by their mother church with its patron, the British bishop, Ninian.

For the period between Ninian and the arrival of Columba virtually the only available evidence for the ecclesiastical history of the Picts is dedication material and a few late legends attached to the *Lives* of Irish and Welsh saints. The situation is much the same for the immediately post-Columban period and the difficulties involved in using this evidence will be discussed later.

COLUMBA

Columba was born in Donegal about 521. He belonged to an important family and as the great-grandson of a king was, by the Irish Law of inheritance, himself an heir to the kingship of Tara. According to Adomnan's *Life,* from the first his parents intended him to enter the Church. As a young man he is said to have attended several of the famous Irish monastic schools, becoming first a deacon and then a presbyter. Many foundations of churches and monasteries in Ireland are assigned to the next phase of his career and he was an experienced churchman by the time he left Ireland.

In later sources there is an overtone of scandal concerning Columba's departure. Adomnan says simply, 'In the second year after the battle of *Cul-Drebene,* the forty-second year of his age, Columba sailed away from Ireland to Britain, wishing to be a pilgrim for Christ'. Adomnan often uses the dates of battles to express chronology and there seems nothing sinister in his reference to *Cul-Drebene*. Later writers, however, believed that Columba had provoked this battle between the north and south, and that, feeling himself responsible for considerable loss of life, had imposed a penance of exile upon himself. There is no hint of this drama in Adomnan. For him the departure to Britain was due simply to the desire to adopt a particular way of spiritual life with a few like-minded friends.

One consequence of Columba's arrival in Britain was that he became *de facto* head of the Church in Dalriada. Columba must have been aware of this likelihood from the first, but Adomnan nowhere implies that this was a prime motive.

Whatever his exact motives – and it is possible that they were to some extent mixed – there is certainly no suggestion in Adom-nan or the later Irish sources that Columba regarded Iona as primarily a mission station from which to convert the heathen kingdom of the Picts.

Plate 12

According to Adomnan, Columba, on leaving Ireland, went first to visit Conall, the son of Comgall, the king of Dalriada, and from there he proceeded to Iona. As we have seen, Adom-nan has nothing to say on the question of the donation of Iona to Columba. The Irish *Annals* say that it was Conall who gave the island to Columba, presumably during this first visit. Bede, on the other hand, states clearly that the donors were the Picts. Columba, he writes, 'brought that nation to the faith of Christ. Therefore he received from them that island, to hold it for the making of a monastery.' Bede had access to good sources for his material on Iona and in spite of their being indications that Bede's sources for the Columban mission included Pictish ma-terial, it is unlikely that he would have failed to correct any Pictish bias in this matter. As an earlier, disinterested commen-tator, his evidence for the donation carries greater weight than that of the Irish annalist.

Historians usually reconcile the two accounts by assuming

that both kings had some say in the donation, but the evidence as it stands is contradictory and an important corollary hangs on the identification of the donor. If we accept Bede's account, then we must also accept the course of events which, taken with Adomnan, it implies. Given these two sources, it would seem that Columba went to Dalriada and from there proceeded to convert the Picts, at least in the sense that Bridei, king of the Picts, received him and gave him permission to preach to his people. As an act of courtesy, or perhaps at the specific request of Columba, Bridei gave him Iona. Bede's date for the con-version of the Picts is 565, so that Columba may have spent as long as two years on the mainland before settling on Iona. If Bridei and Conall both ratified the donation, then the conver-sion of the Picts equally belongs to the first years of Columba's stay in Britain. If, on the other hand, we reject Bede's account, then the Columban mission to the Picts could have taken place at any time during Columba's occupation of Iona.

It has, in fact, recently been suggested that Columba might not have visited the Picts until after the great Council of Druimm Ceta, near Derry, in Ireland, at which Columba played an im-portant part. This would postpone the conversion of the Picts until after 575. The suggestion is based on a close reading of Adomnan's text and the details of the argument cannot be dis-cussed here. Central to it, however, is the belief that Adomnan knew of only one visit by Columba to the Picts, made when Columba was an old man. But an alternative interpretation of the material is possible.

Adomnan seems to have had access to a lengthy chronological narrative which dealt solely with Columba's first visit to the Picts. Incidents from this are scattered through the *Life,* either in groups or singly. This narrative is characterized by the use of the expression 'in the province of the Picts'. In spite of its detail this material is of little historical value being almost entirely made up of hagiographical cliché.

A second series of incidents would seem to refer to subsequent visits to the Picts and these are characterized by the use of the phrase, 'across the ridge of Britain', by which the mountain chain Druimalban is intended. These, without exception, are much more circumstantial; there are convincing topographical details and the incidents themselves are of an individual and unstereotyped character. Incidents of this kind would be quite out of place in the context of the account of the first visit to the king at his royal fortress by the Ness, and must presumably refer to visits made by Columba on later occasions to other Pictish districts.

If this division of the material relevant to the Picts in Adom-nan is acceptable, then the textual difficulties encountered in accepting the traditional view of the early conversion of the Picts are resolved and Bede's explicit testimony on this point need not be discarded.

What results did the Columban mission achieve in Pict-land? The most satisfactory answer to this question is that they were such that Adomnan could write towards the end of the seventh century that Dalriada and the kingdom of the Picts had escaped a prevalent plague thanks 'to Saint Columba, whose monasteries, placed within the boundaries of both peoples, are down to the present time held in great honour by them both,' and that Bede writing thirty years later could say of Iona that its 'monastery was for a long time the chief of almost all those of the northern Scots, and all those of the Picts, and had the direction of their people.'

Unfortunately neither Adomnan nor Bede name a single Dalriadic or Pictish Columban foundation. One possible ex-ception, *Airchartdan,* modern Urquhart, has been proposed by the recent editors of Adomnan. On the basis of the name form there is at least a possibility that there was a Columban monast-ery there, one which could have provided Adomnan with in-formation concerning Columba's mission to the Picts.

Although the Irish *Annals* have a number of entries referring to foundations of Columba's contemporary, Comgall of Bangor, in Dalriada, there is no record of any Columban foundation there. Two entries may concern a Columban monastery in Pictland. At 622 the death of Vineus, 'abbas *Neir*' is recorded, and at 678 the 'dormitatio Nectain *Neir*'. It has been suggested that *Neir* etymologically could represent *Deer,* the name of an ancient parish in Buchan, Aberdeen. In that event the medieval claim that there was a monastery there founded by Columba and his disciple Drostan is considerably strengthened.

The exact nature of Columba's missionary activity is left very vague in Adomnan. In Bede, Columba converts the 'nation' by his preaching and example and 'they' give him Iona. The natural implication, however, is that *Bridius,* 'the most powerful king of the Pictish nation', was the agent in these matters. In Adomnan, on the other hand, we are told simply that Bridei honoured Columba for the rest of his life because of his respect for Columba's powers as a miracle-worker. The silence in Adomnan concerning Bridei's baptism and the donation of Iona has yet to be explained satisfactorily. It is possible that Bridei gave Columba permission to preach to his people but refused baptism for himself, as Bede tells us the Mercian king Penda did in the last two years of his life.

For the rest, the few incidents recorded by Adomnan show Columba preaching 'through an interpreter' and baptizing individuals and households. For some reason these conversions never lead to a gift of land, a pattern so common in later *Lives* of Irish saints.

In 635 Bishop Aidan came from Iona to Northumbria to convert the Northumbrians at the request of their already Christian king, Oswald. Bede admired Aidan greatly, and he gives a full account of his activities in the *Ecclesiastical History*. The facilities given to Aidan by Oswald must have been very different from those provided for Columba seventy years before by

Bridei, but the circumstances of the conversions cannot have been altogether different.

Aidan, like Columba, had to use interpreters and he had a great many Irish helpers with him who preached and baptized throughout Oswald's kingdom. At first the Church in Northumbria was entirely manned by Irishmen, but at once Aidan set about training native clergy. Early in his mission he selected twelve Northumbrian boys for instruction, one of whom, Eata, eventually became abbot of Aidan's own monastery at Lindisfarne.

As far as is known, no bishop to the Picts was appointed by Columba, so no episcopal see comparable with Lindisfarne can have been established in the Pictish area. Bede describes how churches were built in several places and royal money and lands given for the building of monasteries. These early churches were made of timbers covered with wattle – a traditional method of construction which would certainly have been adopted for Pictish foundations and which adds to the difficulties of the archaeologist in the work of locating churches of the Columban period.

DEDICATION EVIDENCE

Frustrated by the lack of detail in the foreign sources, and deprived of the normal native sources for church history many writers have chosen to rely heavily on what can be called the dedication evidence in order to provide some sort of narrative account of what was happening in the Pictish Church in the intervals between the known landmarks of the fifth-century Ninianic mission, the sixth-century Columban mission and the eighth-century Romanization of the Columban Church in Pictland. The justification put forward for the use of this evidence is the belief that it was the regular practice of the Celtic Church to name their churches after the founder. The affiliation, later fixed either by formal dedication or place-name, of a pre-Reformation church site to a Celtic saint is therefore taken as a 'guarantee apart from any records, of personal work at the site'. Armed with the formula: dedication equals personal foundation, it has been possible for historians to construct in considerable detail the missionary activities of Celtic saints in the sixth to the eighth century thoughout the Pictish area.

There is no doubt that the role of the founder was a very important one in the Celtic Church. The church was dedicated to God and the founder's relics venerated at the side of his chief foundation. Abbots were considered to be the legal as well as the spiritual heirs of the founder abbot. A saint's minor founda-tions were collectively known as his *familia* and this grew with the later acquisitions of his successors. An early association with the founder himself, however, brought prestige to the minor foundation and undisputable rights of exaction to the mother church. The result was that the growing power of a foundation carried along with it the extension of the personal effectiveness of the saint, that is, his biography was expanded to coincide with the growing territorial prestige of his 'familia'. Apart, therefore, from the usual gap of centuries between the date of the lifetime of the founder saint and the date of the first written record of the dedication, there was, even in the earliest period, a good reason for a founder to be venerated at a church which had no historical personal connection with the saint of any description.

The whole problem of the valid use of dedication evidence has been given a more hopeful turn for the Dark Age historian by E. G. Bowen in his *Settlements of the Celtic Saints in Wales*. He admits that the majority of dedications are late but that they represent 're-culting' of the saints in areas where 'ancient tradi-tions' of the work of the historical saints have survived. Professor Bowen has demonstrated his theory in connection with the Celtic Church in Wales and if the principle could be shown

to apply in Scotland, then there is perhaps some hope of estab⁄
lishing the usefulness of this material for the ecclasiastical histor⁄
ian of the Picts.

The fact remains that Scottish calendars of Saints are full of
Irish names and that many of the dedications of parish churches
in Scotland are to Irish saints. Where did these commemora⁄
tions come from if they are not relics of Irish missionary activity
in Pictland during the Age of the Saints? It seems reasonable
to conjecture that the great bulk of the dedications are simply
one aspect of the way in which Irish influence after AD 850
swamped the national identity of the Picts. By this period
normal dedications to saints, in the Roman manner, would
be customary, and churches built under the new Dalriadic
administration would naturally be dedicated to Irish saints.
This would explain one feature of the dedications and the
Scottish Calendars, namely, the virtual total lack of recog⁄
nizably Pictish saints. It seems improbable that the Church in
Pictland should have produced no native clerics worthy of
commemoration, as the late dedications suggest. If the Celtic
dedications came into being after the period of the Pictish supre⁄
macy in the north, then the lack of Pictish dedications is more
understandable.

If we are to believe Bede, all the monasteries in the Pictish
area were Columban, a statement which gains importance from
his careful qualification, 'almost all', when referring to the mon⁄
asteries of Dalriada. This monopoly, together with the lack of
any principal monastic centre among the Picts themselves, may
have somewhat depressed the native element in the Church.
Iona may have kept a fairly firm hold on the Columban Church
in Pictland, particularly after the defection of Northumbria,
and have continued to supply at least its leaders throughout its
history.

Some of the dedications may, therefore, preserve useful hints
of the locations of Celtic foundations in the otherwise obscure

period immediately after 850. Others will be due to affiliations and partisan enthusiasms of much later, or possibly earlier, periods. Each dedication requires its own proof of early, or at the very least lack of reasonable motive for later, origin.

Although at the present time virtually nothing is known of the organization of the Columban Church in the Pictish area itself, the impression given by the casual references in Adomnan and Bede is that it flourished as a perfectly normal part of the Celtic Church. There is no hint of any period of apostasy or special idiosyncrasy. At least in this matter the Picts seem to have been thoroughly conformist.

THE EASTER CONTROVERSY

During the seventh century bitter controversy arose between the Celtic Church and the Roman Church, centred on Canter-bury, concerning the method of calculating the date of Easter and the form of the monastic tonsure. One part of the highly technical calculation of the Easter date involved the finding of the date of the Spring equinox and this was done by means of a cycle of recurring years. At one time the Roman Church had used a cycle of eighty-four years, but later, after many amend-ments, a nineteen-year cycle was found to give more accurate results. The remote Celtic Church failed to make the change and continued to use the old eighty-four-year cycle.

In Northumbria the divergence produced the awkward situa-tion of King Oswiu, under the direction of the Bishop of Lin-disfarne, celebrating Easter when his wife, Queen Eanfled, and her Kentish priest were still in Lent.

In order to obtain a ruling on the matter, Oswiu presided over an ecclesiastical synod at Whitby in 663. As Bede reports the speeches, it is clear that the Celtic Colman's stolid affirma-tions that 'the Easter which I keep, I received from my elders, who sent me here as bishop' were no match for the patronizing brilliance of the performance of Wilfred, the Roman spokes-man. The representatives of the See of Peter without difficulty prevailed over 'that Columba of yours'.

The thirty years of 'the episcopacy of the Scots among the English', as Bede describes it, included the eight-year period when at least part of the southern Pictish area had been occupied by the Northumbrians. With Colman in charge of the Church in Northumbria the Columban Church in the occupied area can have suffered no disturbance. The decision at Whitby, however, would effect those Pictish churches also. Bede, writing of the time just after 669, describes Wilfred as occupying 'the bishopric of York, and of all the Northumbrians, and likewise of the Picts'. With Wilfred as bishop to the subjugated Picts there can have been no question of the celebration of the Celtic Easter being tolerated in their churches. Three years after Wil-fred's deposition in 678 a bishopric for the Picts was created at Abercorn on the south shore of the Firth of Forth, with Trum-wine as the first bishop.

There is no hint in any source of the reaction of the native churchmen to the Northumbrian reform. We can suppose that the majority of Pictish clerics resented bitterly this imposed change; but some may have welcomed it, either because of per-sonal conviction on the matter, or because of the perception that by embracing the larger Roman allegiance the church in Pictland could throw off the Irish Columban dominance and at last stand on its own feet.

The resounding victory of Bridei, son of Bili, at the battle of Nechtanesmere in 685 must have, at least temporarily, set aside such thoughts. The Northumbrians in Pictland were, accord-ing to Bede, either killed, imprisoned or enslaved. Trumwine and his monks fled south from Abercorn to find shelter in other monasteries. An intense Celtic revival, with a rejection of all things Northumbrian, must have taken place in the Church as elsewhere and we can assume that the Easter of 686 was celebrated throughout Pictland at a date fixed by the traditional eighty-four year cycle.

The Roman cause, however, soon gained another victory. In 686 Adomnan, then ninth abbot of Iona, had gone to Northumbria on a political mission. He returned there two years later and on this second visit, under the influence of Ceolfrith, abbot of Bede's monastery, Monkwearmouth and Jarrow, he accepted the validity of the Roman Easter. On his return to Iona he failed to persuade the community there to make the change. He had more success in Ireland, however, and by the end of the seventh century the majority of the northern Irish churches accepted the Roman Easter reckoning.

Bede devotes a lengthy chapter in his *Ecclesiastical History* to the Roman reformation of the church in Pictland which took place around 710. The change, as Bede reports it, was entirely the work of the king of the Picts, Nechton, son of Derilei. The most remarkable feature of the whole account is the fact that the role of Columba and Iona in the Church history of the Picts is entirely ignored on both the Pictish and Northumbrian side. It is as though the Columban Church ruled from Iona did not exist. Nor does Nechton mention in his message to Ceolfrith any distinguished cleric, native or foreign, who has influenced his mind on the matter. Nechton and his nation have been 'under an error' and he, Nechton, has decided to renounce it. He requires irrefutable arguments to 'confute those that presume to keep Easter out of the due time', so that in spite of possessing 'much information in these matters', he has sent messengers to Ceolfrith for help. He also wishes for architects to be sent north so that they can build a church for him in the Roman manner, that is of stone, and this he will dedicate to St Peter. Not a backward glance is cast at Columba.

Ceolfrith sent the architects, and with them a long letter starting impressively, 'Domino excellentissimo et gloriosissimo regi Naitano Ceolfrid abbas in Domino salutem'. Bede gives the full text of the letter, which was prepared by Bede himself for Ceolfrith. After an intricate examination of the arguments for the Roman observance, Ceolfrith says that he will not send nineteen-year cycles since Nechton had said that he 'had enough of those Catholic tables concerning Easter'. The acceptance of the change by Adomnan, 'abbot and renowned priest of Columba' is mentioned, but with no recognition that the attitude of an abbot of Iona was of special relevance to the Picts. The letter ends with the admonition that Nechton 'make the nation observe in all points the things that pertain to the unity of the Catholic and Apostolic Church'.

According to Bede, the letter was read in the presence of the king and his most learned men after it had been translated into Pictish. By his 'royal authority' Nechton ordered the suppression of the old cycles and the adoption of the nineteen-year cycles 'throughout all the provinces of the Picts to be transcribed, learned and observed'. The tonsure was also to be changed, 'and the nation thus reformed, rejoiced as being newly put under the direction of Peter, the most blessed Prince of the apostles, and secure under his protection'.

It is not known what influence had brought Nechton to the Roman side of the Easter question. It is most probable, as has been suggested, that the nucleus of a Pictish Roman faction was formed during the Northumbrian occupation. Copies of the nineteen-year cycles were no doubt left behind in the Pictish churches of the occupied area, and it may be to these that Nechton refers in his message.

It is reasonable to suppose that there was an underlying political motive in Nechton's action. The recent fighting on the southern frontier of his kingdom may well have caused Nechton to review his political situation and he may have seen that a Northumbrian alliance would be much to his advantage. According to Adomnan, the boundary between the Picts and the Irish in Dalriada at the end of the seventh century was the

Dorsum Brittaniae, the Spine of Britain, the chain of mountains running from Cape Wrath in Sutherland directly south. The Picts had therefore lost ground in the north-west since the days of Columba and Bridei, son of Maelcon. Such a motive for the Pictish mission to Northumbria might account for the direct approach from the Pictish king and the pointed ignoring of his Irish connections.

Whether or not Nechton had hopes of political advantage from his approach to the Northumbrians, Bede's account certainly gives the impression that Nechton now regarded himself as the head of the Pictish Church and that he was totally rejecting the authority of the Columban Church directed from Iona. Easter and the method of tonsuring were changed, but that was not to be all. He clearly had a major disruption in mind.

Persuaded by Egbert of Northumbria, the Roman Easter was at last accepted by the monks of Iona in 716. For the following year the Irish *Annals* record the 'Expulsion of the *familia* of Iona across the Spine of Britain by Nechton the king'. Bede's account definitely implies that Nechton had imposed his will in these matters well before 716, so that the *Annals* entry, if it is not misplaced, suggests either the expulsion of a dissenting minority, or more probably, a complete removal of Columban personnel who refused to recognize his authority in the affairs of the church.

THE REFORMED PICTISH CHURCH

After the dramatic glimpse of the Pictish king surrounded by his most learned men, Pictish ecclesiastical history again becomes obscured, and confused post-medieval material is all that remains in the way of sources. We do not know how the new, truly Pictish Church flourished after its inauguration by Nechton. It is not known where the stone church was built. If it was built, and there is no reason to suppose that it was not, then presumably it became the administrative centre of the new Church. To cover this period in his *Celtic Scotland,* Skene, attracted by the emphasis on dedications to St Peter and the prominence given to the activities of a king called Nechton, relied on late legends concerning the sixth-century Pope Boni-face. Skene's arguments depend on a chain of identifications none of the links of which are capable of bearing much strain. On the basis of his analysis of this material, Skene claimed Rosemarkie in Ross-shire as the place where the stone church was built, but this is by no means proved, and a site in the south is what one would naturally expect.

More recently it has been suggested that Nechton, as part of his reorganization of the Church, established a regional bish-opric at Abernethy in Angus. The fifteenth-century Bower makes the interesting observation in his *Scotichronicon,* that Aber-nethy was the chief royal and episcopal seat of the Picts and that there had been three elections of bishops there when there was only one bishop in Pictland. The evidence is not good, being late and uncorroborated, but Bower does claim to have had access to a chronicle of the church of Abernethy and it is just possible that it contained early authentic material.

There is a record of an 'episcopus Scotiae Pictus' attending a council in Rome in 721. This has usually been taken as a reference to an Irish bishop of Pictish birth but it could equally well be a Pictish bishop of Irish birth. The presence of some representative of the Pictish Church at Rome at this period would be appropriate.

There is therefore a trace of evidence that the Pictish Church under Nechton, as one might expect, was losing its largely monastic character and moving towards the Roman system of a Church centred on regional episcopal sees.

The best evidence for thriving Christianity in the eighth century is the large number of sculptured stones found through-out the Pictish area, which bear on one side of them elaborately decorated crosses. We can assume that these monuments were commissioned by Christian patrons, and the stylistic ornament and iconography employed for the most part come from an ecclesiastical background of a lively and receptive kind. Opinions vary as to the exact date of these cross slabs but they were almost certainly erected after the Romanization of the Pictish Church.

Nechton's reign ended in a period of unprecedented political confusion. At least until Oengus, son of Fergus, had established himself on the Pictish throne, church affairs must have remained very much in the background. Ceolfrith addressed Nechton as 'devout king' in strong contrast to Oengus's Northumbrian epitaph, 'tyrannical murderer'. Nevertheless, while obviously in no sense a saintly king, Oengus might reasonably, as a matter of prestige, have seen fit to endow a royal foundation of his own.

The name Oengus, son of Fergus, is given in two late legends as the founder of St Andrews in Fife, the church which from the tenth century at least, became pre-eminent in Scotland. Whether the famous eighth-century king is intended or the ninth-century king of the same name is, however, not clear.

The use made of these legends by Skene cannot be discussed in detail here but two of his speculations have gained such wide acceptance that they should be mentioned.

In the legends, a St Regulus brings the relics of St Andrew to the Picts and he, together with the king, Oengus, son of Fergus, founds the church of St Andrew. Skene would identify this Regulus with an Irish saint, Riagail of Mucinis, a contemporary of St Columba. The identification is based chiefly on the closeness of the feast days of the two saints. Bishop Dowden confuted this argument convincingly at the end of the nineteenth century, but the article in which he did this has been forgotten and Skene's identification continues to be used. Skene further believed that Riagail's foundation was established at the time when St Cainnech had a hermitage in the same place, Cainnech's association with Kilrymont (St Andrews) is based on a very late gloss to an Irish martyrology and is not acceptable as contributary evidence for a sixth-century Christian community in the district.

The second of Skene's hypotheses calling for comment is his belief that the church dedicated to St Andrew was established in place of the Celtic monastery by Acca of Hexham during his period of exile from Northumbria sometime after 731. Hexham was dedicated to St Andrew, and Acca a noted collector of relics, so that Skene suggests that it was Acca and not Riagail, the founder of the Celtic monastery, who brought the relics of St Andrew to Pictland. There are many objections to this theory, the chief of which is the fact that there is no record of a dedication to St Andrew at Kilrymont before the tenth century. The presence of Acca in Pictland at all is merely speculation and without the St Andrew dedication the aptness of the Acca connection loses its force. Moreover, had Acca been the founder, it is highly improbable, that he would have been so entirely forgotten at St Andrews. Acca was an important churchman whose memory was secured for ever in the writings of Bede.

Nevertheless the name of Oengus, son of Fergus, was given to the Pictish king associated with the foundation of St Andrews, and this has to be accounted for. If the later, more obscure, Oengus is intended, then the likelihood that a genuine tradition has been preserved is perhaps greater. Otherwise, the compelling ecclesiastical motive of desiring to establish seniority may be at work. The antiquity of the foundation would be well established if a Pictish, as opposed to a Scottish, connection could be demonstrated, and the selection of the most celebrated king of the Picts as founder of the most celebrated church in Scotland has an air of plausibility. Such a claim would be very useful in confrontation with any rival claim to seniority from, say, Dunkeld.

There are two pieces of evidence concerning the early history of the church in St Andrews which are of undoubted value. First, the Irish *Annals* record in 747 the death of an abbot of *Cennrigmonaid,* (Kilrymont). This abbot is often described as an abbot of St Andrews, but there is no reference to St Andrew in the entry. Skene thought of him as the last abbot of his hypothetical Celtic monastery founded by Riagail. We know, therefore, that there was a monastery at Kilrymont during the reign of Oengus, son of Fergus. It is, of course, merely a random entry. There are no regular entries concerning Pictish foundations in the *Annals*. He could have been a first abbot, a last abbot, or an abbot in the middle of a succession.

Plates 62–64

The second piece of evidence is the imposing tomb-shrine commonly called the St Andrews Sarcophagus. Art-historians tend to seek backing for their stylistic dating of the ornament on this monument from the written records. In fact the historian stands in much greater need of the results of the art historian. Opinions as to the date vary from the eighth century to the tenth. The present writer favours the eighth century and produces arguments in support of this in a later chapter. The magnificence of the shrine implies that the monastery which contained it was an important one – so important indeed that it might well have been under the patronage of the reigning king Oengus, son of Fergus. There is no way of telling, however, whether or not the monastery at Kilrymont was founded by him.

The later versions of the list of the Pictish kings attach the note 'He built Dunkeld' to King Constantine, son of Fergus, who reigned from about 789 to 820. This has been interpreted as an attempt by a king who had reigned in both Dalriada and Pictland to inaugurate a common ecclesiastical centre which would bring about a mutual reconciliation of the two peoples. Unfortunately the only evidence associating Constantine with Dunkeld is this one very late note. The ecclesiastical notes attached to the later versions of the king list are in general of very little value, being based on late legendary material of the type discussed in connection with Boniface and Regulus.

It is generally assumed that Kenneth, son of Alpin, refounded Dunkeld after he had defeated the Picts around 850. In the Scottish Chronicle he is said to have transported the 'relics of St Columba to a church that he had built'. The name of the church is not mentioned although later in the account of his reign the Danes are said to have 'wasted Pictland to Clunie and Dunkeld', which perhaps implies that the Danes were attracted by the prospect of a wealthy ecclesiastical foundation at Dunkeld.

The first explicit reference to Dunkeld occurs in the Irish *Annals,* where under 865, the death of a cleric described as abbot of Dunkeld and first bishop of Fortriu, is recorded. The meaning of 'first' in this context has been shown convincingly to imply 'chief' as opposed to 'first in time'. The title, therefore, implies the pre-eminence of Dunkeld over a number of other bishoprics in the combined kingdom of the Picts and Scots. That the abbot of Dunkeld was also a bishop carries a Celtic overtone which is entirely suitable to this period. Dunkeld, with its relics of Columba, its chief abbot-bishop, and its control over both Scots and Picts, was as near to a re-creation of the hey-day of Iona and the Columban Church in the sixth century as the age could allow.

The end of the Pictish Church as reformed by Nechton seems to have come at the end of the ninth century when the reigning king 'gave liberty to the Scottish Church, which was in servitude up to that time after the custom and fashion of the Picts.' Whatever the exact nature of this servitude, it sounds as if the Pictish kings had maintained Nechton's position as the controlling authority in Church matters.

The history, in the sense of a continuous record of development and change, of the church in Pictland can scarcely be said to exist. The total lack of native sources combined with the poverty of the information to be found in foreign sources has meant that neither its foundations nor its clerics have left their mark. The careful examination of late written source material for authentic detail may begin cumulatively to produce new light on the Pictish church, but archaeology provides the best prospect for increasing knowledge in this field. The recent spectacular excavation of St Ninian's Isle in Shetland has revealed the foundations of a pre-Norse and therefore potentially Pictish church. The gradual accumulation of such finds is the only way in which Pictish Church history can be built up on a factual basis freed from the tangle of bias and speculation to which, in its own way, each succeeding age has contributed.

CHAPTER IV

The End of the Kingdom of the Picts

IN 761 OENGUS, son of Fergus, the most powerful of all the kings of the Picts had died. Although he had failed utterly to achieve his ambition to gain control of the Britons of Strath-clyde, we have seen that there is no reason to suppose that during his lifetime he lost control of his earlier conquest, the kingdom of Dalriada. One hundred years later a Dalriadic leader, Ken-neth, son of Alpin, was on the combined throne of the Picts and Scots of Dalriada and the Picts had for ever lost their in-dependence. How this total reversal of Pictish fortunes came about can only be guessed at, for the sources for this last phase of Pictish history are very few indeed. The Irish *Annals* stop using material from the Iona Chronicle at about 750, so entries concerning Dalriadic and Pictish affairs appear much less fre-quently thereafter. For some reason which is difficult to explain, there are more entries concerning the Picts than the Scots, for the 750-850 period. Bede's *History* came to an end in 731 and the continuation of his chronological recapitulation fails after 766. Even the lists of the Pictish kings and the lists of the Dal-riadic kings both present problems for this period. The order of succession and the lengths of individual reigns can be estab-lished with reasonable certainty up to about the middle of the eighth century but after that discrepancies occur, discrepancies which cannot be checked by reference to other sources. An ac-count of the last hundred years of Pictish independence can therefore only be a skeletal affair with no guarantee that such bones as have survived are the vital, structural ones.

The later version of the Pictish king list, described as List 2, gives an account of the Pictish succession for the period im-mediately after Nechton, son of Derilei, which differs appreciably from that found in the earlier List 1. These discrepancies have either been dismissed as the fictions of scribal corruption or claimed as historical evidence for the existence of native pretenders or regional kings during and immediately after the end of Oengus' reign. There is no doubt that all the versions of List 2 are very corrupt at this point, but it is possible to detect the nature of the corruptions and to reconstruct with fair certainty the appearance of the original list from which all the versions are taken. When, however, this emended text is compared with List 1 the differences are found not to be those of scribal corruption. Nechton, son of Derilei, for example, is given two reign lengths, one corresponding to that given to him in List 1, and the other, a short reign of nine months, which as we know from the Irish *Annals* was in fact correct. Nechton's reign is therefore dealt with in more detail and with greater accuracy in List 2 than it is in List 1. The most dramatic difference is the ascription of a reign of sixteen years only for Oengus himself in List 2 in contrast with the thirty years given to him in the earlier list. The Irish *Annals* imply a reign of about thirty years for Oengus but the entry concerning the weakening of his authority in 750 may have at least some relevance here. There is no doubt that Oengus died king of all the Picts and there seems to have been no difficulty in his brother succeeding him; but it may be that after the serious defeat of 750, when his army was at its weakest, rival claimants to the throne of the families of Nechton, Drust and Alpin came to the fore. More probably perhaps, the compiler of List 2 may simply have found a place in his list for regional leaders who were of importance during this period. From the eighth century century onwards the Irish *Annals* do occasionally refer to regional Pictish kings. Certainly List 2 at this point ceases to be consecutive.

An argument against the authenticity of the names is that no trace of any of them is to be found in other sources, but this is true also of certain names in List 1 for this period. The lateness and the corruptness of the versions of List 2 make certainty impossible. But if the end of Oengus's reign was characterized by the appearance of rival claimants or even of a growing regional independence, then the kingdom of the Picts had an internal weakness which could have contributed to its later collapse. The discrepant Lists provide, however, the only evidence that could be interpreted as indicating that Pictland was a less united country in the late eighth century than it had been in preceding centuries.

Bridei, the brother of Oengus, who had succeeded him, died after a short reign of two years, the last of the remarkable family of Fergus. He was succeeded by a certain Ciniod (Kenneth) – at least according to List 1, for this king does not appear at all in List 2. In 768 the Irish *Annals* record the fighting of a battle in *Fortriu* between Aed and Kenneth. The result is not given but the fact that the battle was fought on Pictish ground suggests that Aed was the aggressor.

This Aed was Aed Finn, son of Eochaid, who is given a reign of thirty years in the lists of Dalriadic kings and whose death is recorded in the *Annals* at 778. When Aed first came to the throne, he must certainly have been answerable to Oengus, and for lack of evidence to the contrary we must presume that he remained so at least until the death of Oengus's brother in 763. In these circumstances the battle of 768 could be interpreted as a revolt.

Aed must have succeeded in throwing off Pictish dominance eventually, for according to the good evidence of the Scottish Chronicle the Rights and Laws which the Scots imposed on the new combined kingdom of Picts and Scots were the Laws of Aed. This perhaps suggests that Pictish Laws had been introduced among the Scots by Oengus and that Aed repudiated them, substituting a Dalriadic code of his own. We might assume therefore that Dalriada regained the independ/ence it had lost at the hands of Oengus some time before Aed's death in 778.

It becomes increasingly difficult to understand the relation/ship between the two peoples after the reign of Aed Finn. The lists of the Dalriadic kings are very confused due to misplace/ment and other scribal corruptions. Those lists which appear most reliable from the point of view of the order of the succes/sion are not so trustworthy for reign lengths and the Irish *Annals* provide few checking points. What the sources seem to indicate, however, is that a Donald, son of Constantine, reigned in Dal/riada for twenty/four years beginning some time in the eighties, while his father Constantine, son of Fergus, reigned in Pictland from about 789 to 820. Constantine himself reigned in Dalriada for the last nine years of his reign, his son presumably having predeceased him. If the lists of the kings, for both countries, are to be believed, this must mean that the Picts and Scots were united under Constantine and that the Picts had restored the *status quo* of Oengus's reign.

Constantine had fought his way to the Pictish throne in 789, overthrowing Conall, son of Tadg. This battle is described in the *Annals* as a 'battle among the Picts', so there is no doubt that Constantine was a Pictish leader in control of the Scots and not the other way round, as has been suggested.

To add to the confusion, the king whom Constantine over/threw seems to have reigned afterwards somewhere in Dalriada. He was later killed in Kintyre by another Conall who also be/came 'king'. These two Conalls must be regarded as pretenders during the reign of Donald.

It is to this same king Constantine, son of Fergus, that one of the versions of List 2 of the Pictish kings ascribes the build/ing of the church of Dunkeld. Even though the note is late and so of little value, there is a certain appropriateness in the choice of location for a ruler of both the Picts and Scots. The founda/

tion is attributed elsewhere to Kenneth, son of Alpin, when he was in a similar political position.

Constantine's long reign, therefore, saw the recovery of Pict-ish authority in Dalriada after the period of revolt led by Aed Finn. But it saw also the introduction of a new element in the political situation, for the Viking raids had begun. In 794 the Irish *Annals* record the 'Devastation of all the islands of Britain by the heathens'. The following year Skye and Iona were at-tacked. In 802 Iona was burned and four years later sixty-eight monks of the community killed. The activities of the Vikings undoubtedly played an important part in steering events towards the Pictish catastrophe both directly and indirectly. Viking attacks on North Britain were coming from all sides, making it inevitable that the native element, comprising both Picts and Scots, should concentrate in the heart of the area – in Pictland itself.

In 820 Constantine was succeeded by his brother Oengus. According to the Pictish lists Oengus reigned for twelve or fourteen years; in the Dalriadic king lists he is given a reign of nine years and his son Eoganan a reign of thirteen years. In the Pictish list Eoganan is given a reign of three years, following the joint reign of Drest and Talorgen which occupied the three years immediately after Oengus's death. Although there is con-siderable difficulty in making sense of the various reign-length attributions, it looks as though we have here another case of a Pictish king setting his son to rule over Dalriada.

Eoganan's death is recorded thus in the *Annals* at 839: 'A battle by the heathens against the men of *Fortriu* and in it fell Eoganan, son of Oengus, and Bran, son of Oengus, and Aed, son of Boanta'. The leaders who fell were presumably fighting together. Aed was a Dalriadic king so there may have been a Pictish-Dalriadic alliance; on the other hand he may have been taking his orders from Eoganan. Eoganan occupies in some respects a unique place in Pictish history; he is the first certain example of a king of the Picts whose father was also a king; he is the only Pictish king, as far as is known, to be killed by the Norse; he is the last Pictish king whose death is recorded in the Irish *Annals*.

Nothing at all is known of the means whereby Constantine had re-established Pictish control in the west and set his family on the throne for fifty years. This family must have had considerable talent both as fighters and as administrators but it has been their misfortune to lose all claim to fame through the failure of the sources. In List 1 only two kings follow Eoganan: Uurad, son of Bargot, who reigns for three years, and Bred who reigns for one. This would give the year 843 for the end of the Pictish kingship. List 2 gives Uurad, here in the form Ferat, a three-year reign also, but Bred, identified here as a son of Ferat, a reign of one month only. There then follow three additional names, two of which are also sons of Ferat, and these three reigns total six years. This would make 849–50 the date of the overthrow of the Picts, and many later sources do in fact use 850 as the date for the commencement of the union of the Picts and Scots. A note is attached to the last king named in List 2 saying that he was killed at Forteviot 'but according to others at Scone'.

According to the Irish *Annals* Kenneth, son of Alpin died in 858. The tenth-century Scottish Chronicle, which provides the most trustworthy account of Kenneth's career, begins, 'So Kenneth, son of Alpin, first of the Scots ruled this Pictland prosperously for sixteen years.' This would make Kenneth's reign as king of the Picts and Scots begin about 842–43, which agrees with the account in List 1. There is no hint in the Chronicle of any substantial part of the reign being spent in the actual subjugation of the Picts.

In the thirteenth-century Chronicle of Huntingdon Kenneth's reign is described as commencing with much fighting against the Picts. On one occasion 'he fought seven times in one day with the Picts' and five years passed before he had 'confirmed the kingdom to himself'. The lateness of the Chronicle of Huntingdon as a source for this period gives the account little authority but it is noticeably less imaginative than the other late versions of the overthrow of the Picts. Certainly one very possible interpretation of the presence of extra kings in List 2 is that they represent Pictish leaders who made a last stand against Kenneth of the kind described in the Huntingdon Chronicle. The fact that no less than three sons of a Pictish king are themselves listed as kings suggests that in a period of confusion, dating perhaps from the reign of Eoganan, the more constitutional methods of selecting a king had given way to expediency. The last three names in List 2 may belong simply to national leaders rather than to formal kings.

The other late accounts of the end of the kingdom of the Picts which are attached to certain versions of the king lists may be conveniently mentioned here. They tell in dramatic terms how the Scots, 'far inferior in every way', by treachery overcame the Picts who were 'far superior in arms and courage'. The treachery is variously described. In some versions the Scots come secretly armed to a general council; in others, in timehonoured fashion they encourage the Picts to eat and drink overwell and then kill them off when they are incapable. In these stories the Pictish king is Drust, the last name in List 2, and it is from two versions of them that the annotator of the list has got his information. These accounts are only of interest in so far as they show a proPictish, or rather antiScottish bias in their writers. It is perhaps of significance also that the writers felt some surprise at the defeat of the Picts by the Scots and thought it appropriate to invent some explanation of how this came about.

For further facts concerning the overthrow we have to return to the Scottish Chronicle. There Kenneth is said to have been king of Dalriada for two years before he came to Pictland. In some of the Dalriadic king lists this period 841–843 is assigned to Kenneth's father Alpin. Little is known about Alpin. It was the name Alpin which caused some of the scribal corruption of the lists with much resulting confusion about his reign length and its dates. There was a tradition, which probably belongs to him, that an Alpin was murdered in Galloway after he had 'destroyed' it. The Huntingdon Chronicle claims that Alpin himself had achieved a considerable victory against the Picts but that he had been defeated and killed by them the same year. There is no hint in any other source, however, that Kenneth was carrying on a campaign inaugurated by his father.

Most unfortunately the passage describing the circumstances of Kenneth's accession to the Pictish throne has been omitted by the compiler of the material in the manuscript which contains the early Scottish Chronicle. All that remains is the following statement: 'Pictland was named after the Picts whom, as we have said, Kenneth destroyed. For God deigned to make them alien from, and void of, their heritage, by reason of their wickedness; because they not only spurned the Lord's mass and precept, but also refused to be held equal to others in the law of justice.' Though this has obviously been written by a Scottish cleric who wished to squash the authority of the Pictish Church, his statement that the Picts were 'destroyed' and had lost 'their heritage' is important.

How did Kenneth achieve his position as king of the Picts and Scots? For some reason there is no contemporary notice in any foreign source about this major change in the balance of power in North Britain. It is very difficult indeed to understand why, for example, the Annals of Ulster should record the fighting between the Picts and the Norse in 839 and the death of Kenneth in 858 and yet omit all mention of the history-making events which intervened. Unless it is a matter of chance merely, the only conclusion would seem to be that while the events did make history, and they did so very quickly in this case, their true significance was not realized at the actual moment of oc-curence. In the *Annals* Oengus's annexation of Dalriada was followed battle by battle but there is no record of Constantine's similar achievement. Fighting between the Picts and Scots in the ninth century was perhaps too common an affair to be worthy of special attention, particularly when the clerical re-corders were so understandably preoccupied with the activities of the 'heathens'.

There seems no doubt, however, that something fairly dra-matic must have occurred. In all the sources the emphasis is on Kenneth's being the 'first of the Scots', 'the first king from among the Gaels that assumed the kingdom of Scone'. This provides further proof that the joint reigns over the Picts and Scots by fathers and sons in the late eighth and early ninth cen-turies were controlled from Pictland. Eoganan was the fourth king of the Picts to occupy both thrones. Kenneth's position as the first of the Scots to control the Picts is therefore understand-ably remarkable.

On the evidence available, Kenneth fought his way to the throne of the Picts. The Scottish Chronicle of 150 years later says that he 'destroyed' the Picts, and had any rights in the matter of the kingship existed they would most probably have been made the most of. The Scottish Chronicler goes out of his way to emphasize the complete severance of the Pictish heri-tage brought about by the accession of Kenneth. It has often been suggested that Kenneth might have had a claim to the Pictish throne through his mother and that the three additional kings in List 2 represent rival claimants. If this were the case, then the failure of the Irish *Annals* to record even one encounter in a campaign which lasted from 843 to 850 becomes very surprising indeed. Moreover, one would certainly expect the kingships of Dalriada and Pictland to separate again on Ken-neth's death, for an eight-year reign would scarcely have been long enough to reconcile all parties to a permanently combined kingship for the Picts and Scots. The last three names in List 2 would seem most probably to be those of agitators rather than serious rivals to Kenneth, but proof is lacking.

Eoganan died in 839 when he was, as far as the king lists can be interpreted, in control of both the Picts and Scots. Any victory of 843 must be related to this fact. Both Pictish king and Scottish subject-king died in the battle of 839, so a show of force from one side or the other was inevitable. A war of aggression in Fortriu had once before succeeded in putting an end to the Pictish régime and it is possible that Kenneth had a similar move in mind. In 839 many of the men of Fortriu had fallen 'almost without number', so that the Pictish fighting force had been considerably weakened. The interpretation of events offered by the Chronicle of Huntingdon seems very reasonable; 'when Danish pirates... with the greatest slaughter had destroyed the Picts who defended their land, Kenneth passed into the remaining territories of the Picts.'

The word 'destroyed' used in the Scottish Chronicle taken at its fullest meaning implies the complete destruction of the Pictish army and its leaders, followed up by a general devasta-tion of the country. At this period of history a disastrous defeat of this type often meant a temporary loss of independence for a nation. Some such catastrophe must have lain, for example, behind the Northumbrian occupation of part of Pictland in the seventh century. Oengus's 'percussio Dalriatai' of 741 is also directly comparable. The actual military achievement, there-fore, although impressive, particularly in its dramatic reversal of the roles of the two nations, was not in itself so out of the ordinary as to compel the attention of foreign scriptoria.

The long-term results of Kenneth's success were, however, very different from anything that had happened before to either the Picts or the Scots. About thirty years after Oengus's con-quest the Scots revolted successfully against the Picts, and it took the same time for the Picts to throw off the Northumbrians. Why was it the Picts did not recover from this blow also?

There is probably no single straightforward explanation for the final nature of Kenneth's conquest, but one major contrib-utory cause must have been the fact that the Scots did not simply occupy part of Pictland or control all or some of it through a subject king – they took it over completely for themselves. The list of the Pictish kings comes to an end about 850 but so does the list of Dalriadic kings. There are no more independent kings of Dalriada. After the fighting the entire secular and ec-clesiastical administration with the king at its head appear to have abandoned Dalriada and moved into Pictland. It is as though Oengus in 741 had moved the Pictish court to Dunadd or Dunolly.

Kenneth's war may have begun as a revolt, achieved an an-nexation and ended up as a migration, but it is perfectly possible that settlement was what the Scots had in mind from the first. The kingdom of Dalriada was very cramped, bounded by the mountains of Druimalban on the east and on the south by the powerful kingdom of the Britons of Strathclyde whose affairs were closely watched by the even more powerful Northumbria. Moreover, their awkwardly narrow-shaped territory was moun-tainous, making communications difficult, and much of it was unsuitable for habitation and cultivation. An eastward expan-sion of the kingdom, if it hoped to develop at all, was inevitable and only the strength of the Picts had contained this movement so long. Even so, it can probably be assumed that at all periods there was considerable peaceful penetration of Pictland by groups of Scots. The presence of well-established Scottish settle-ments may have dictated, for example, the choice of Scone for the new capital and Dunkeld for the chief church.

Dalriada's territorial position had worsened during the first half of the ninth century. The Norse settlement of the Hebrides constricted the kingdom even further and brought these marauders uncomfortably close. The necessary abandonment of Iona may have suggested the idea of removing the civil seat of power also into a position of greater safety. If the re-settlement of Dalriada in the heart of Pictland was premeditated, then it was a brilliant idea brilliantly timed to be carried out just when the Picts were least able to defend themselves. What happened, in southern Pictland at least, may well have resembled the dealings of Aethelfrith of Northumbria with the territories of the Britons which Bede describes as 'driving the inhabitants out and planting English in their places'.

Something in the nature of a mass migration of Scots from the west into the east about this time would account for the swiftness of the collapse of the Picts – their early loss of identity and language. What the Scots did to Pictish Argyll in the fifth century they did to the rest of Pictland in the ninth. It is often noted that the title 'king of the Picts' and references to 'Picts' go on in the Irish *Annals* until the beginning of the tenth century, but this can scarcely imply any particular Pictish vitality. Fairly quickly the Picts must have had to reconcile themselves to being a subject people in their own country, for throughout the remainder of the ninth century both peoples had to concentrate on survival in the face of relentless attacks from both west and east by the Scandinavians. There is no likelihood, however, that the combined kingdom of the Picts and Scots represented a union of equals for the common good with mutual respect for institutions. To confirm the Scots in their role as rulers of the Picts it was necessary for them to suppress the characteristically Pictish activities of their subjects in a systematic manner. There is a record of the substitution of Scottish ecclesiastical and civil laws for the existing Pictish systems and it can be supposed that similar substitutions in all walks of life were also insisted upon.

The collapse of the kingdom of the Picts was therefore ultimately due to the disturbance of the political balance in the north brought about by the Norse settlements. From about 800 the Picts were losing lands in the far north, and the Scots lands on the west coast; so, whatever their previous relations, a struggle to the death between these two peoples who were being compressed into the central Pictish area was inevitable. The Picts, preoccupied with defending themselves against the Norse, failed to realize the greater menace from the west, and the initiative taken by the men of Dalriada won for them the kingdom of the Picts and a lasting place in the future history of north Britain.

CHAPTER V
Pictish Art

As THE ONLY SUBSTANTIAL native relic, the monumental art of the Picts has particular value. It is, however, far from being merely of archaeological interest for it is, on any terms, of considerable technical skill and high aesthetic value.

The sculptural art of the Picts, as it has survived, exists only as a means to convey a highly organized system of symbolism. For some reason, bound up presumably with the meaning of the symbols, the Christian symbol of the cross could be placed aptly alongside them, so producing a Christian art which can take its place with other contemporary manifestations of Christian art in neighbouring countries. But the fact remains, that the message of the symbolism was the prime motive for the erection of these monuments and not the message of the Christian Church. A selection of the commoner symbols is illustrated here, the most common of all being the crescent with an applied V-shaped rod, the double disc with an applied Z-shaped rod, and the symbol often called 'the swimming elephant' – though it will be described here as the 'Pictish beast'. The symbols are remarkably stereotyped, to a degree which makes it almost certain that we are dealing with symbolic and not merely decorative designs.

Fig. 12

A series of animal designs is associated with the abstract symbols and doubt has been expressed as to whether these are truly symbolic, carrying a meaning other than the mere depiction of an animal. The probability is that they should be considered as symbols. Where they are repeated they too are stereotyped in design, the most dramatic example being the numerous repetitions of the Burghead bull. Symbols are not found alone but a single symbol can be accompanied an animal, which then appears to serve as a symbol. Animals, on the other hand, do

Fig. 13

Fig. 12. Pictish symbols from Class I stones

appear singly. An important link between the abstract designs and the animals is the fantastic Pictish beast which is articulated with scrolls and lobes in exactly the same way as the naturalistic animal designs.

Pictish sculptures were collected, classified and analyzed by J. Romilly Allen in *The Early Christian Monuments of Scotland* at the beginning of this century. His work remains a mine of information on all aspects of the stones. He grouped the monuments into three classes. Class I comprises simple, roughly dressed stones and boulders with the characteristic symbols incised upon them. The technique of incision varies; it can be a neat V-shaped cut, a rounded scoop or a percussed line. Whatever the technique and however hard the stone, the incision is made in the majority of cases with a masterly assurance. Of the many examples which illustrate the skill of the Pictish sculptors the symbol stone at Golspie is perhaps the most remarkable for the sensitivity and control of its lines. Unfortunately no photograph can do adequate justice to this exquisite craftsmanship. The stone at Dunnichen and the reverse side of the Glamis Manse stone, both in Angus, provide further typical examples.

Plate 31

Plates 28, 30

Class II comprises carefully dressed stone slabs of varying height, breadth, and thickness. On these, an interlace cross occupies the whole of one face, the background being filled in with a mixture of iconographical material. In nearly every case the symbols appear on the opposite side to the cross. Often they are very large and prominently displayed at the top of the slab but there are many examples where a great number of small symbols are scattered in amongst other representations. Typical of the class are Aberlemno Churchyard, and Eassie, both in Angus.

Plates 40–43

The earliest of the cross slabs are carved in very shallow relief, a technique particularly suited to Pictish artists, for the delicacy and accuracy of their line is displayed to better advantage with the slight raising of the image. Later the relief became much

Fig. 13. Pictish animal symbols from Class I stones

higher, until at the end of the series the figure sculpture is virtually three-dimensional as, for example, the angels on the great
Aberlemno roadside stone.

Plate 58

Fig. 14. *Terminal rings of Pictish silver chains: a. Whitecleuch, Lanarkshire. b. Parkhill, Aberdeenshire.*

Romilly Allen's Class III contains sculptures obviously related in manner to Class II but omitting altogether the symbols. Class III belongs, in all probability, to the period after the end of the independent Pictish kingdom; it will only be mentioned incidentally here.

A few examples of Pictish symbols have been found in contexts other than standing stones. A symbol was scratched on a bone found when excavating the Broch of Burrian, North Ronaldsay. In the far north also, symbols have been found on circular sandstone discs. They appear on two leafshaped silver plaques and on a silver hand pin found in the Norrie's Law, Fife, hoard. Two of the terminal rings belonging to examples of the remarkable series of Pictish silver chains have symbols engraved on them. The engraving on these pieces exhibits a technical mastery and extreme delicacy of line exactly similar to that found on the sculptured monuments.

Only a drawing remains of a crescentshaped bronze plaque bearing other symbols, found in a brochlike structure at Monifeith.

Symbols appear, finally, incised on the walls of caves at Covesea, Elgin and East Wemyss, Fife. There remains the possibility that symbols appeared on perishable materials such as cloth, leather and wood but no fragment exists to afford proof of this. The only surviving wood carving of possibly Pictish date are

Plates 16, 18

Fig. 14

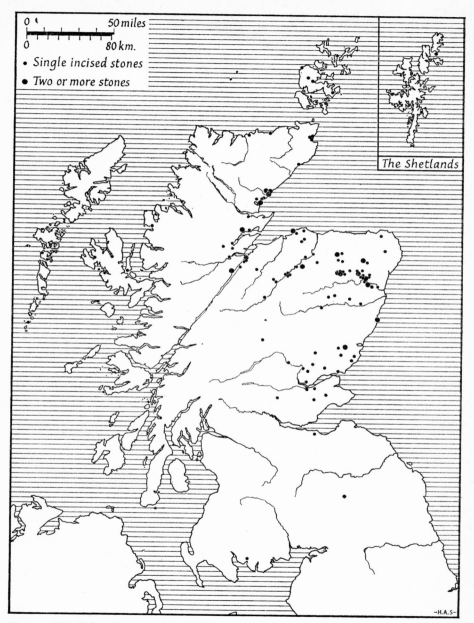

Fig. 15. *Distribution of stones incised with Pictish symbols (Class I)*

The Shetlands

0   50 miles
0   80 km.

• Single incised stones
● Two or more stones

–H.A.S–

Plate 17

the abstract patterns which decorate the sides of the interesting wooden box from Birsay, Orkney. It has been suggested that the tools which it contained are those of a leather worker.

Fig. 15

Fig. 16

Examples of Romilly Allen's Class I appear in the west of Scotland in districts such as Skye and the Hebrides but Class II is not represented there. Class I monuments are distributed over the whole of the Pictish area after the establishment of the Scottish colony in Argyll, from Shetland in the north to Perth-shire in the south. Class II, on the other hand, reflects the state of affairs described in Adomnan's Life of *Columba* where the boundary between the two peoples at the end of the seventh century is given as the *Dorsum Brittaniae,* the mountain chain, Druimalban, which runs from Cape Wrath directly south. The distribution, therefore, confirms what is on all counts probable, namely, that chronologically the monuments of Class I pre-ceded those of Class II, though some of the former may still have been erected after the introduction of the latter.

It has frequently been noted that Class I predominates north of The Mounth, whereas Class II is more numerous in the south. The natural implication is that Class I, and so the prac-tice of erecting symbol stones, began in the north. This type is found in the north in three concentrations: on the shores of the Moray and Dornoch Firths, down the Spey corridor and up the Don-Urie valley. Joseph Anderson, whose Rhind Lectures on the stones form the introduction to Romilly Allen's cata-logue, thought that the most likely centre of origin for the stones was in Aberdeenshire where the simple type of monument is most prolific. The present writer has argued for an origin in the most northerly area of concentration, the shores of the Moray and Dornoch Firth, the crux of the argument being the higher

Fig. 17
Plate 29

quality of the stones in this area and the inflation of the Aber-deenshire numbers by debased examples which are probably of late date.

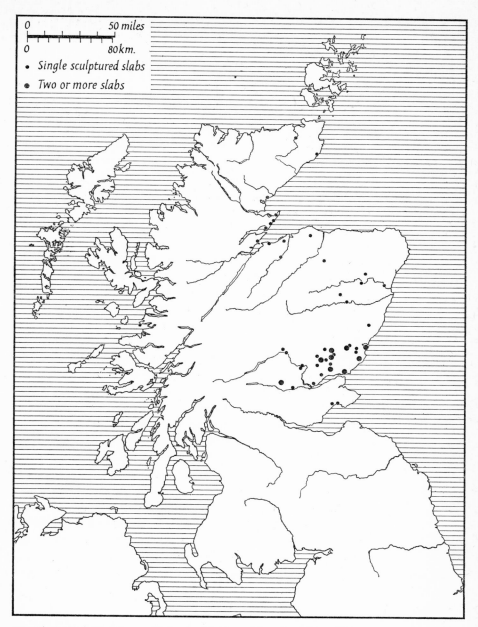

Fig. 16   Distribution of cross slabs bearing Pictish symbols sculptured in relief

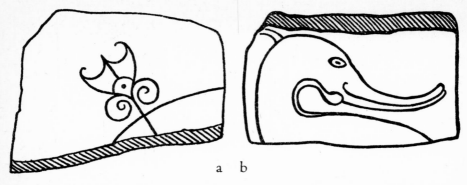

a   b

Fig. 17.   Two northern fragments of Class I stones: a. Terminal of V-rod, Little Ferry Links, Sutherland. b. Head of Pictish Beast, Inveravon, Moray

From the days of the *Caledonii* of Ptolemy the Moray Firth area seems to have been of importance. It is tempting to associate the dissemination of the symbolism with Bridei, son of Mael-con, who, as we have seen, had a royal fortress on the River Ness, and who had wide authority. The political unity implied by the distribution of the symbol stones certainly points to a figure of the stature of Bridei as its originator, but most writers would consider him too early to be associated with the symbol stones. Another candidate, whose date is more suitable, is Bri-dei, son of Bili, the great liberator of the southern Picts whose territories had been occupied by Northumbria from about 655 to 685. In this context the symbols might be interpreted as an expression of nationalist feelings originating in the free north, and subsequently spreading to the south after the departure of the Northumbrians.

Before passing to a more precise consideration of the dating of the monuments something must be said about a recent ad-vance in the study of the designs of the symbols. This is the *Fig. 18* principle of what may be described as the 'declining symbol'. Briefly, it recognizes the existence of a correct form for each symbol and postulates that this correct form is in the main rep-

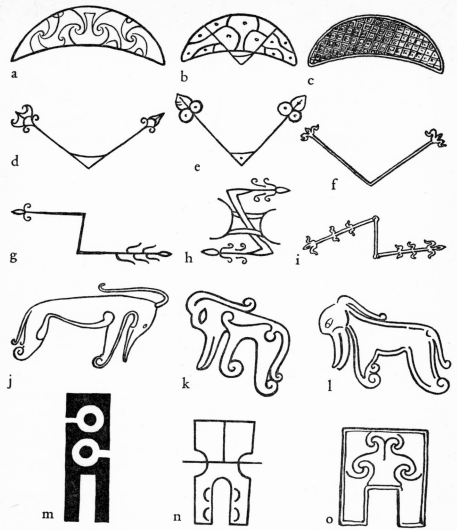

Fig. 18. The declining symbol: a. Golspie, Sutherland. b. Kintore, Aberdeenshire. c. Monifieth, Angus. d. Clynemilton, Sutherland. e. Kintore, Aberdeenshire. f. Monifieth, Angus. g. Norrie's Law, Fife. h. Anwoth, Kirkcudbright. i. Monifieth, Angus. j. Golspie, Sutherland. k. Fyvie, Aberdeenshire. l. Largo, Fife. m. Whitecleuch, Lanarkshire. n. Mill of Newton, Aberdeenshire. o. Aberlemno, Angus

resented by the earliest examples, and any decline from it, by later examples. This feature of the Pictish designs was noticed first by R. B. K. Stevenson in connection with the infilling of the crescent, and the present writer has found that an examina‑ tion of other symbols, including the Pictish beast, has produced similar correct forms. Whatever objections may be raised to the general principle of interpreting a typological series as a chro‑ nological one, in the particular case of the symbols it is justifi‑ able, for we have a set of later‑in‑time designs with which to check the progress of the series – the designs of the symbols on the Class II monuments. For example, examination shows that there is a correct form for the terminals of the V‑rod involving a fish‑tail terminal and an arrowhead terminal, as at Clynemil‑ ton in the far north. In the Kintore example this distinction of terminals has been ignored and we find the same thing in such late examples of Class II as the Hilton of Cadboll cross slab. It seems reasonable, therefore, to suppose that the passage of time which has caused this detail to be ignored in the Class II stone was also responsible for the Kintore simplification. As a further check on the proposition that the Kintore symbol is a late example the treatment of the infilling of the crescent is also bro‑ ken down. When, therefore, we see that the terminals on the Mo‑ nifieth plaque crescent are identically treated, the plaque can be taken as belonging to the later period of the history of the monu‑ ments. Again the infilling treatment is in agreement, Steven‑ son's correct pelta and scroll designs having been abandoned entirely. The usefulness of such an approach is obvious. For example, the incised symbol found carved on natural rock at Anwoth, Kirkcudbright, has sometimes been used to argue the presence of Picts in this area at some period. The similarity of the terminals of the Z‑rod on the double disc symbol makes it quite clear, however, that the symbol was incised at a period when we know there was no Pictish settlement in Galloway. It can therefore be safely dismissed as an outlier.

The decline of two other symbols, the Pictish Beast and the notched rectangle, is illustrated here; the pictures speak for themselves. At Golspie the scrolls are applied with understanding to the body of the creature and are an integral part of the design; at Fyvie they meander meaninglessly across the body, while at Largo, a Class II monument, they have declined into a mere double lining. The notched rectangle of the terminal ring of the Whitecleuch silver chain is a fascinatingly complex design. At Mill of Newton a dull symmetry has taken over, and the design has been further smoothed away on the Class II Aberlemno Churchyard slab.

THE DATE AND STYLE OF CLASS I

Joseph Anderson presents the classical argument for the date of the erection of Class I stones in his Rhind Lectures. Bede, he says, expressly states that the Picts were the original possessors of the territory afterwards occupied by the Dalriadic Scots. The symbol stones, which are not found in this area, must therefore post-date this settlement. The only objection to this argument is the unanswerable one that symbol stones may yet turn up in this area. One real difficulty is that it is by no means certain when the Dalriadic settlement, in contrast to casual small-scale immigrations of Scots, actually took place, though some time in the second half of the fifth century is currently accepted as the most likely period. If we add to this Adomnan's account of the later Scottish-Pictish boundary mentioned above, we have a date for Class I lying between about AD 500 and 700.

Dating by association of the symbols with other phenomena is more complex. The northern sandstone discs and the bone from the Broch of Burrian were not found in any clear stratification. The Broch of Burrian finds, however, came from a secondary occupation level and the presence of a Celtic bell on the site indicates a period of occupation continuing at least into

Christian times. The excavation of the Sculptor's Cave, Covesea, Moray, revealed a Bronze Age occupation and a later re-
occupation from the second to the fourth century AD. The symbols incised on the walls have been associated with this later
occupation but it cannot be proved that this small group of
perfunctory symbols, was executed by the actual occupants of
the cave. They could be the *graffiti* of temporary users of the
caves, such as fishermen, in any period. The East Wemyss caves
present a much more convincing picture of caves decorated by
the actual inhabitants. In a recent detailed and careful study
Mr Charles Thomas carries over the Covesea secondary
occupation date to these southern caves and their carvings,
which include some of the symbols. He admits, however, that
at least one of the representations, the dog from Jonathan's
Cave may possibly be intrusive, and by implication belong
to a later period. This considerably weakens the argument,
for if one representation is intrusive, then any could be – the
Pictish beast, for example, in the same cave. The dog in question,
is in fact of mannered design suggesting a seventh century date
at the earliest.

The objects found in the Norrie's Law hoard ought to help
to provide a date for the Class I symbols but unfortunately the
dating of the objects bearing the symbols, and even the date of
the deposition of the hoard, are disputed. R. B. K. Stevenson
would date the plaques and hand pins to the seventh century.
Mrs Fowler prefers a sixth-century date.

Such inscriptions as there are on symbol-bearing stones do
not provide any very significant information about date. There
are two miniscule inscriptions in the vernacular, one at For-
doun and the other at St Vigeans. Professor K. H. Jackson dates
them to the eighth and the ninth century respectively, which
provides useful checking points for the dating of the Class II
monuments. Class I stones have Ogam inscriptions only, and
these, as we have seen, are in a version of the Ogam alphabet

Plate 26

to be dated to the eighth century. This proves that Class I stones such as those at Brandsbutt and Logie Elphinstone, both in Aberdeenshire, were still being erected in the eighth century, if not later.

The representations on the symbol stones themselves do not provide significant information concerning date, although an expert analysis of the material culture which appears in connection with the figure sculpture on the Class II stones has yet to be made. The presence of the cross in Class II imposes a date some time after the conversion in the mid-sixth century. An apparently Roman tonsure on a cleric depicted on a St Vigeans stone suggests a date after 710, when this tonsure was first introduced among the Picts. Mr Stevenson has suggested that the female rider on the Hilton of Cadboll stone is holding a penannular brooch but there is not sufficient detail in the design to allow us to date it. It has frequently been remarked that in Class I the mirror symbol is a representation of a late La Tène mirror type but Mr Stevenson would explain this as due to native continuity and cites examples of the same process in connection with other objects.

Some of the Class I symbols were once held to represent stylized versions of objects carried in Roman Triumphs, seen from the front and side, suggesting a Roman context for the origin of the symbol designs, if not for the practice of erecting symbol-bearing monuments. More recently a case has been made out for some of the symbols representing similarly oddly viewed stylizations of the impedimenta of the Celtic warrior aristocracy of the first century AD. Again, of course, the implied date refers to the designs as such, and not to the Class I monuments.

In the present writer's opinion definite information about the dating of the Class I symbol stones can best be obtained by comparing the incised animals with animal designs which occur in certain highly important Dark Age art monuments from outside the Pictish area, namely (1) the gold jewellery of a pagan Anglo-Saxon king, unearthed in 1939 from the ship-burial mound at Sutton Hoo in Suffolk, and (2) the sequence of luxury Gospel books produced in monasteries situated somewhere in these islands in the seventh and eighth centuries.

The royal treasure of Sutton Hoo was buried ceremoniously with the king's long ship sometime before the final conversion of the East Anglian nobility, that is, around the mid-seventh century. The gold jewellery, of the utmost sumptuousness, was made by a workshop of master jewellers presumably some time in the first half of the seventh century. The king's purse cover is ornamented with stereotyped animal designs, an eagle pouncing on a duck, twice repeated, a man between two rampant lions, also twice repeated, and a great central motif of four long-bodied fantastic animals whose jaws and fringed feet are drawn out into a complex tangle. These fantastic animals, with their fluent outlines, narrow waists, drooping necks and trailing stylized legs and feet are strikingly close to the design of the formalized Pictish beast.

Fig. 19

Fig. 20d

The garnet and gold shoulder clasps from Sutton Hoo are each decorated with two pairs of boars, interlocked and radi-

Fig. 19. Beast from the Sutton Hoo purse cover

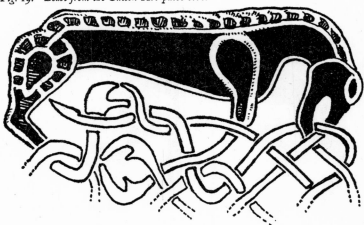

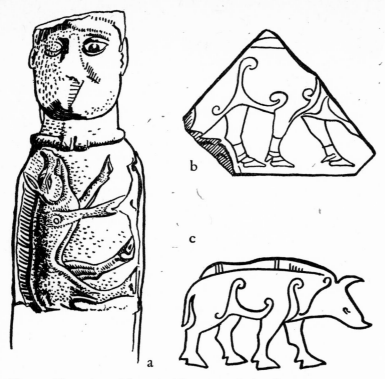

Fig. 20. Comparisons of boars: a. The Boar God of Euffigneix (Haute-Marne), Gallo-Roman period. (After Pobé). b. Dores, Inverness-shire. c. Knocknagael, Inverness-shire. d. Conjoint boars on Sutton Hoo shoulder clasps

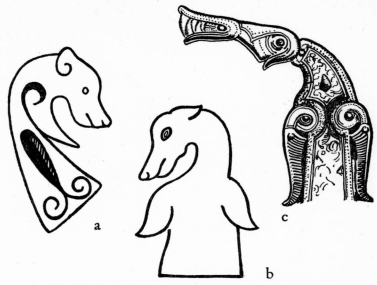

Fig. 21. 'Beast head' symbols compared: a. Norrie's Law, Fife. b. Rhynie, Aberdeen-shire. c. Sutton Hoo Shield, head of finned dragon

cally formalized. These boars with their high crests of bristles, heavy sloping shoulders and heads, and the detailed, if stylized, treatment of their snouts and hooves, again provide a close analogy for the massive outline of the Knocknagael boar and the neat detailed drawing of the hooves of the boar of Dores. To this collection of boars we may add, for visual comparison only, the treatment of the Gallo-Roman Boar God of Euffigneix.

Fig. 20 c
Fig. 20 b

Fig. 20 a

On the Sutton Hoo shield there is a gilt-bronze dragon-like creature, whose tapering body is articulated by pairs of wings or fins. The general appearance of this beast, with its vividly described head poised on a strong neck and its cramped in-drawn flippers, offers the best formal parallel among Dark Age artifacts for the curious beast portrayed on the Pictish Rhynie stone and the Norrie's Law plaques.

Fig. 21

Animal designs, some realistic and some fantastic, which offer a number of parallels to Pictish designs, were therefore part of the repertoire of metalworkers serving an English royal patron in the first half of the seventh century. Beyond speculating whether the English and the Pictish animal designs may not have shared some common ancestor, Roman or British, and whether the English designs may have influenced the Pictish ones or *vice versa,* we could not push this comparison further, were it not for the vitally important fact that the art of the Sutton Hoo jewellery leads us without any perceptible break to the decoration of the earliest of the great seventh-century Gospel books, namely, the Book of Durrow, preserved in the Library of Trinity College Dublin. There has been much debate as to whether English or Celtic scribes wrote and illuminated the Book of Durrow. However, the discovery of the Sutton Hoo treasure made the argument for an English origin of this book difficult to counter.

The ornamental page which precedes the Gospel of St. John in the Book of Durrow has a central design of interlace strands, interspersed with circular ornaments, which speaks the same bold decorative language as the Sutton Hoo gold buckle. The circular ornaments amidst the interlace contain stepped patterns, comparable to the step-sided gold cells for garnet inlay on the studs, buckles and other jewels of Sutton Hoo. The side por-tions of the St John preface page contain tangled lithe-bodied beasts with long jaws and fringed feet identical to those on the Sutton Hoo purse, and consequently, close in feeling to the Pictish beast.

Fig. 22

Fig. 22. Book of Durrow, biting beasts.

In the Book of Durrow appear the four Evangelist symbols, the Man of St Matthew, the Lion of St Mark, the Bull of St Luke and the Eagle of St John. These symbolic creatures are each depicted on a separate blank page, surrounded by a thick ornamental frame. The lion is a wolf-like animal, and closely resembles the rampant lions on the Sutton Hoo purse. Everything about St John's eagle is of the nature of metalwork. It is stiff, static, segmented just as a jeweller would build up his image out of gold cells and inlaid stones. The eagle is in fact a coloured drawing of a Sutton Hoo-type jewel, and could reasonably be attributed to the workshop of the master jeweller, not now working to illuminate the person of a pagan king, but instead the Gospel of the Lord of the Universe. The eagle's wings hang weightily at his sides like the fins of the dragon on the Sutton Hoo shield.

The Durrow illustrations of the Evangelist symbols differ from the Evangelist pictures in the later Lindisfarne Gospels, and also from the earlier illustration of St Luke in St Augustine's Gospels, a famous and influential book brought from Italy to Canterbury around 600, in that they show, not a portrait of the saint accompanied by his symbolic creature, man, eagle, lion, bull, but the symbolic creature alone. So the St John or St Luke pages in the Book of Durrow do not belong to the naturalistic Mediterranean tradition of the Lindisfarne Gospels and the St Augustine Gospels, but to something distinct and independent, and presumably native to Britain. This other, native, tradition can be traced back to the agressively stiff animal designs set off against the white spaces of the Sutton Hoo ivory purse cover, or equally to the Pictish symbol stones. At Ardross, Knocknagael, Grantown, a wolf (or boar or stag) pauses, as it were, in motion across the clear upright rectangle of the stone.

This general analogy between the animal on the stone and the Evangelist symbol on the page can be further particularized. The lion of Durrow has features which correspond closely to

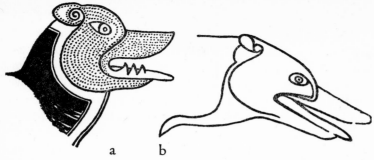

Fig. 23.   Comparison of animal heads: a. Book of Durrow, Lion of St Mark. b. Ardross, Ross-shire, wolf

the Pictish wolf – the specific manner of drawing the ear, and *Fig. 23* the segregation of the muzzle from the cheek, and above all the great spiral infilling of the neck, shoulder and belly. But we must note that this lion is a painting of a hard metal jewel. The spiral patterns on the animal's body have become stiff cells to hold, as it were, agate plates in position, whereas the long loops and scrolls which the Pictish artist so exquisitely traces across the body of the Ardross wolf express with masterly ease and *Fig. 24*

Fig. 24.   Comparison of the use of spirals on foreleg joints of the Durrow lion and the Ardross wolf

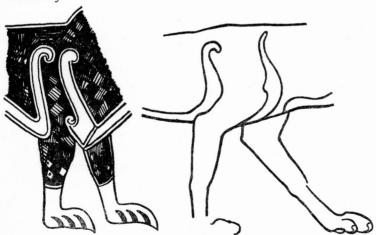

Fig. 25

knowledge the shimmering muscular strength and swift lollop-
ing stride of a living beast. Later, the Ardross wolf type paces
across the Book of Kells, but now the articulating spirals have
become gestures merely, applied without any understanding of
their original anatomical function.

Both St Mark's lion and St Luke's quietly ambling calf in
the Book of Durrow, drawn in profile on a blank page, with
spirals invading the body at thigh and shoulder, have a definite
stylistic and historical connection with the Pictish incised animals. They have the appearance of Pictish animal designs re-
handled by an artist familiar with metalwork techniques of the
Sutton Hoo, or related, workshops, not necessarily fixed and
resident in East Anglia. It seems possible that Pictish animal
designs, such as that which has survived on the Ardross stone,
were available for study and imitation around 650 and were
first interpreted in terms of Sutton Hoo jewellery, that is, stiff-
ened, formalized, and in effect coarsened.

Between the creation of the illuminations in the Book of
Durrow and the creation of the Echternach Gospels and its
brother codex, Corpus Christi College, Cambridge MS. 197,
no great time can have elapsed. The Evangelist pictures still
show the symbolic creatures only, set in profile on a broad page,
not yet the Mediterranean man and symbolic creature of Lindisfarne. But an important change has taken place both in the
Echternach bull symbol and in the MS. 197 eagle, as compared
with their counterparts in the Book of Durrow. The former
now conform, in all essentials, to Pictish designs. Neither animal
is transmuted into a Sutton Hoo-type jewel, but accurately follows the elgant, linear, but vitally realistic Pictish type of animal
as exhibited in the Grantown stag and Ardross wolf. The in-
Plate 33
terior spirals on the flank and shoulder of the Echternach bull
are used exactly as the Pictish artists used them. And the eagle
of MS. 197 is no longer the odd-looking penguin of Durrow,
but a dangerous preening eagle, ruffling his magnificent plumage

Fig. 25. Book of Kells, wolf

and spreading his fierce talons, exactly – or almost exactly – as we see him in the Knowe of Burrian stone.

Plates 37, 38

Almost exactly – for there is a highly interesting discrepancy between the Pictish eagle and the eagle in MS. 197. When we study the Pictish bird, we see how economically its designer has used his strong curved incisions. An unbroken line runs from the bird's tail, describes the edge of the great feathers of the wing, the curve of the wing on the shoulder, and, returning from a tight hook or spiral at the neck, defines the breast and the foreleg. The designer of the Corpus Christi eagle uses basi-cally the same formula, but gets muddled. By misplacing some elements, extra descriptive lines have to be added. The breast has to be drawn separately, the foreleg also, and the tail becomes all wing feathers. There can be no doubt that the sculptured and the painted eagle are historically related; the discrepancy between them can be interpreted in either of two ways. Either the Pictish sculptor has improved upon, tidied up, and made entirely coherent, a design created by a manuscript illuminator, or else the illuminator, removed in space and time from his Pictish model, has inadvertently drifted away from its exacting standards of draughtmanship.

This pair of alternatives has to be considered in relation to another pair. Is it more likely that Pictish artists should have borrowed formal designs from the limited range of Evangelist symbols produced in monastic scriptoria in the seventh century and then have employed these designs as the basis of a whole race of animals with no iconographical relation to the Evangelists? *Or* that sketched copies – or some other forms of reproduction – of the already extant, independent Pictish animal designs reached the centres of insular Christian manuscript illumination, wherever these may have been, and resulted in the type of Evangelist symbols which we see in the seventh century Gospel Books?

The illuminators both in Echternach and MS. 197 are unhappy about the isolated motif of the symbolic creature on the blank page. The Durrow artist had accepted this, as we have seen, but the later artists poke crosses and geometrical patterns in from the edge of the page, besieging the creature. This is an important aesthetic feature, a criticism of the isolation of the animal, which may have led to the rejection of this primitive type of the Evangelist symbol, and the adoption of the southern portrait type in the next great book of the series, the Lindisfarne Gospels, illuminated in Lindisfarne by the Englishman Eadfrith, before his death in 721.

Whether or not we actually accept the hypothesis of active Pictish influence on the early pre-Lindisfarne development of the Evangelist symbols, we none the less have evidence for the dating of the incised symbol stones. Be it as a cause or as an effect, the Pictish animal designs (and it is axiomatic that the animal designs carry with them the rest of the symbols) are stylistically related to Durrow, Echternach and MS. 197. The dates of these books are not fixed by any definite historical evidence, inscription or colophon, but they are generally admitted to fall into the second half of the seventh century, or perhaps a little before or after. If we take the stylistically tight sequence,

Sutton Hoo – Durrow – Echternach, we are, roughly speaking, dealing with the 625–700 period. There are materials in Sutton Hoo and Durrow out of which the Pictish beast could have been formed. There are other animal designs in both these sources which tie up well with Pictish examples. By the time we reach the comparatively mature elegance of Echternach, we find such exact formal analogies between the work of Pictish artists and the illuminators, that a relationship, a historical contact, is certain. Even if the Picts learned their art from the illuminators and ultimately the metalworkers of the south (and the present writer prefers to see the Picts as the active contributors and teachers), they could have begun their apprenticeship and perfected their own art any time from 650 onwards, that is, during the period of the Northumbrian occupation of part at least of the southern districts of the Picts.

R. B. K. Stevenson has recently analyzed the decorative infilling of the Pictish crescent symbol, and has pointed out metalwork analogies for its interior decoration which indicate a seventh-century date for the creation of this particular symbolic design in its earliest and most complex form. Such a date is in agreement with the suggested dating of the emergence of the animal symbols as set out above.

THE DATE AND STYLE OF CLASS II

Class II brings with it a physical and technical change in the national monuments of the Picts. When the Pictish king Nechton sent his messengers to Ceolfrith of Jarrow, the Ruthwell cross had been standing for a number of years, and it has been assumed that it was contact with a Northumbrian school of relief sculptors which inspired Pictish artists to abandon their simple native technique of incision and attempt to emulate the more sophisticated English products. The heavily plastic, classical style of the Ruthwell and Bewcastle crosses is, however, far

Fig. 26. Golspie, Sutherland. Incised entangled snakes

removed from the early examples of Pictish sculpture in relief
and it is only in the loosest sense, if at all, that such models
could be said to have produced the distinctive Pictish relief style.

The quality of execution in relief sculpture among the Picts
is extremely high. It moves from the shallow exquisitely drawn
relief of Rossie, Glamis, Eassie, and Aberlemno Churchyard
to the plastic modelling of Aberlemno Roadside and the magnificent stones at Meigle. In the north this technical brilliance is
well represented in the perfection of Hilton of Cadboll and the
extreme complexity of Nigg.

Plates 60, 61

It is important to recognize this development in relief techniques, for in it we can perhaps find the explanation of the
shift by Pictish sculptors from incision to relief. On the earliest
relief monuments there is a mixture of both techniques, and it
can be shown that at this early stage there was in fact very little
difference between them. Indeed we could regard as the first
movement towards relief the inner rolls between the lines forming the scroll on the Burghead bulls, the eye of the fish and
duck of Easterton of Roseisle, and the entangled snakes at the
bottom of the Golspie cross slab. The fact is, if the incision is
sufficiently deep, then the area contained within two incised
lines is virtually in relief. The recognition of this pseudo-relief

Plate 50

Plate 32

Fig. 26

on Class I stones makes the transition to the Class II relief monuments an easy one. The treatment of the triple disc at Glamis is very similar to that of the same symbol at Kintrad- well – incision is used with an emergent area between two deeply cut lines. It has often been remarked that the Picts did not care to copy the freestanding cross of their contemporaries but devised instead a new type of monument – the cross slab. An examination of certain Class I stones themselves (this is an instance where photographs are quite inadequate) shows the earliest relief techniques used by the Picts on their monuments also to be their own invention.

Plate 39

The fundamental difference between Class I and Class II is the presence of the interlace cross, and it seems probable that the change in the nature of the monuments is simply the result of accommodating this new design. The cross needed a regular rectangular field and so the stones had to be cut to this shape. Interlace, to be at all effective, required shallow relief to express the intertwining of the strands and the Picts had a method ready at hand to achieve this. The result is the cut and dressed slab with shallow relief ornament which defines Class II.

Romilly Allen detected thirteen different cross-types on mon- uments belonging to Class I and Class II. One interesting type, omitted by Allen but noticed by R. B. K. Stevenson, is the cross with a quadrilobate, instead of the usual true circular, ring. Rings of this type are found on a group of early monuments otherwise related, and which includes Aberlemno Church- yard and Eassie. Such a treatment of the ring does not occur in Irish or Northumbrian sources but it is found on some of the pre-Scandinavian Manx crosses. In this context, however, it might well be a Pictish borrowing.

Fig. 27

By far the commonest types of cross on Pictish monuments have round hollow angles and double square hollow angles, respectively. The round hollowing of the angles of the cross is common in both Northumbrian and Irish sculpture. The double square hollow type is not found on sculpture; it is essentially a drawn design. Examples of this design are found on ornamental pages in the Book of Durrow, the Lindisfarne Gospels and the Lichfield Gospels. The combination of a ring with this type of cross, which also appears on Pictish sculptures, would seem to be a conflation of sculptural and manuscript models.

The normal treatment of the shaft of the cross is a straight extension of its lower limb, this and the shaft being distinguished by a change of infilling pattern. Such a change of pattern is regularly observed on the Irish interlace crosses of the eighth century.

In a few of the earlier Pictish crosses the shaft is distinguished from the lower limb by notches half as large as the hollowed angle, of whichever type, used at the intersection. A similar arrangement is found on the cruciform page in the Lindisfarne Gospels.

It would seem, therefore, that, as we should expect, the Picts found their cross types from sources similar to those used by Irish and Northumbrian artists. The novelty of the quadrilobate ring, however, suggests that in this matter they were not merely copyists.

Romilly Allen described with painstaking accuracy all the variations of ornament used by the Picts to decorate their crosses but a comparative study of the extraordinary variety of interlace, spiral and key patterns has yet to be undertaken. R. B. K. Stevenson has recognized a typical closely knit type of interlace, and certain local types can be isolated. Allen's pattern 553, for example, is found only in Perthshire and Angus, and stones which for other reasons group together can be shown to draw on the same type of patterns although often in different contexts. Each workshop we can suppose had its own book of patterns.

From the start, Pictish sculptors seem to have had no difficulty in laying out an interlace pattern. Allen's analysis reveals

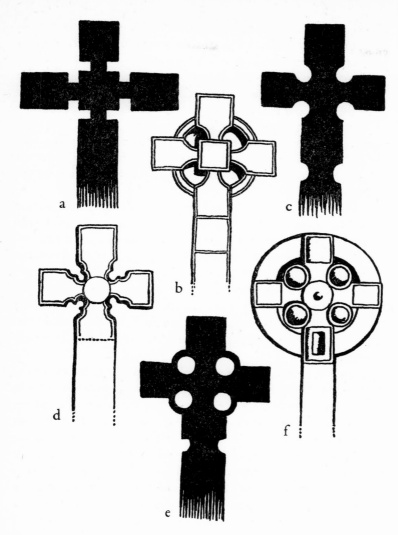

Fig. 27. Pictish Cross types: a. Nigg, Ross-shire. b. St Madoes, Perthshire. c. Glamis 1, Angus. d. Glamis 2, Angus. e. Eassie, Angus. f. Aberlemno Roadside, Angus

no early history of mistakes and coverings-up. Indeed, according to Allen the three large circular knots of the early Glamis
Manse stone are filled with the most elaborate interlace pattern
in sculptured stone work that has survived. Again, the undoubtedly Hiberno-Saxon idiom is being used creatively, so far
as can be judged without knowing the prototype employed.

In general, the Hiberno-Saxon elements in such early cross
slabs as Glamis Manse and Aberlemno Churchyard are of such
high quality that they might seem to show the Pictish sculptors
freely participating in the evolution of the Hiberno-Saxon style.
In which case these elements could have been acquired from
Northumbria at any date after the introduction of the Hiberno-
Saxon style and not, as has been suggested, a generation after
the production of the Lindisfarne Gospels.

It is in fact reasonable to regard the beginning of Class II as
one of the effects of the Pictish-Northumbrian *rapprochement*
brought about by Nechton around 710. Nechton's admiration
for all things Northumbrian has been discussed fully in an earlier chapter. According to Bede, Northumbrian architects did
go north to supervise the building of a stone church for Nechton
and there is time, before Nechton's political downfall, for the
church to have been built. It is easy to imagine Pictish artists
acquiring knowledge of the Northumbrian illuminators' art at
this period and being eager to attempt its transference to their
stone monuments.

Like the rest of the ornament, the crosses on the earliest examples of Class II are executed in very shallow relief. As the
series progresses, the Pictish sculptors appear to have outgrown
their manuscript prototypes, and, in some workshops at least,
come positively to luxuriate in the possibilities of ever-deepen-
ing relief. Pictish art is probably at its most successful when it
owes most to its entirely native talent for the exquisite control
of line, but the monuments in the later, bolder, style are none
the less highly impressive. The flat cross taken, it seems, straight

from a manuscript page is replaced, although not everywhere, by something which is much more akin to the free-standing cross. In scale, and in the proportions of the cross, stones such as Aberlemno Roadside and the Meigle 'Daniel' stone have the architectural presence of standing crosses rather than cross slabs. The abstract decoration on these later monuments is treated three-dimensionally, much use being made of stud and boss prominences. At Aberlemno Roadside the rounded hollows of the angles of the cross are brought forward, and a new ring encloses the top of the cross entirely. At Dunfallandy a typical 'manuscript' cross has its arms decorated with a simple arrangement of grouped studs. At Nigg the cross is covered with normal shallow relief ornament but the background is peppered over with studs formed of spiral ends, and bosses which are in effect blown-up roundels of interlace. The complexity of the Nigg design verges on the decadent, although it must be said that this monument photographs badly; a photograph allows the design to be taken in at a glance and the result is inevitably oppressive. Confronted with the stone itself the eye falls on sections of the design with its breathtaking technical mastery. The surprising thinness of the slab also counteracts the florid effect produced by frontal photography.

Plates 56, 58

Plate 61

The central decorative motif of snakes coiling round interlace-covered bosses, found also on the St Andrews Sarcophagus, closely resembles the decoration of an eighth-century gilt bronze object of Irish origin, where, however, it is used more economically, the coiled snakes themselves providing the emergent roundels.

Plate 64

The Meigle 'Daniel' stone, which is a Class III monument, has a unique cross type. Here the upper segments of the ring form the top of the monument and so the cross is at least partially released from the slab. The studding of the cross arms and the enclosing ring are no doubt inspired by the metalwork convention of decorating surfaces with studs of coloured stones of

Plate 56

enamel such as is found on the Ardagh Chalice. The effect, however, is far from jewel-like, giving instead an impression of reinforcement which adds to the general feeling of massive strength conveyed by this monument.

Crosses on Iona have boss decoration very similar to that found on these later sculptures, and R. B. K. Stevenson has put forward strong arguments for the evolution of the Iona cross boss-style at least partially under the influence of Pictish models. Such influences would have been at work at the beginning of the ninth century, a period which, we have seen, saw the joint rule of the Dalriadic Scots and the Picts by the Pictish king, Constantine, son of Fergus, and his son.

SECULAR ICONOGRAPHY

The cross and its decorative treatment is a field in which comparisons with other Dark Age artistic artifacts can be made, but a remarkable characteristic of the Pictish sculpture in relief is the amount of iconographical material they contain for which no comparable material can be found.

First, of course, there is the symbolism itself. The Class II treatment of the symbols, as has been mentioned earlier, maintains the general outline of the designs but the later sculptors apparently felt quite free to depart from the traditional decorative treatment.

Naturalistic animals also appear in Class II but the extraordinarily forceful animal symbols have become merely animals observed and portrayed with sensitive accuracy. Some of the animal iconography, such as kneeling animals and motifs involving a monstrous creature attacking a domestic animal would seem to point to an ultimately Eastern source but historically likely prototypes are difficult to adduce.

Plate 41

The battle-scene on the back of the Aberlemno Churchyard stone is perhaps the most interesting of the large number of scenes

Fig. 28.   Meigle 26, Perthshire. Two confronted beasts

showing horsemen – principally engaged in hunting – which taken together comprise a remarkable, if not unique, corpus of frankly secular representations, whether based on historical events or literary sources.

We are justified in saying 'if not unique' because there does exist a body of Dark Age sculptured crosses in England and the Isle of Man which carry scenes not derived from Christian tradition and iconography, but from literary sources, so that the iconography is secular. The Gosforth Cross is thought to illustrate the Voluspa poem in the *Poetic Edda*. The cross shaft at Halton in Lancashire, and a group of stones in the Isle of Man self-evidently illustrate scenes from the legend of Sigurd.

The technique of the Sigurd stones is poor, and we cannot suppose that the craftsmen who carved them invented their own iconography. Besides, we are able to produce a specific pictorial source, namely embroidery. No embroidery illustrating the Sigurd legend survives, but literary sources suggest that such embroideries did exist. In the Volsunga Saga, for example, Brynhild is described as seated in her bower overlaying cloth with gold and 'sowing thereon the great deeds which Sigurd had wrought'. In the early eleventh century a scald called Thorfinnr at the court of Olaf the Holy of Norway was ordered to compose in verse a description of the scenes represented on a tapestry in the Hall. The scenes he describes are exactly those shown on our Sigurd stones.

It might therefore be suggested that the other great group of secular scenes on Dark Age sculptured stones, those on the Pictish cross slabs, notably the battle scene at Aberlemno, like-wise trace descent from embroidery designs. The suggestion can only be made tentatively for the analogies date from a period later than the Aberlemno stone, and refer to areas outside Pictish territory. A hanging presented to Ely Minster by Aethelflaed, widow of Byrhtnoth (died 991), is described in an inventory as showing 'the deeds of her husband'. We may presume that this hanging showed Byrhtnoth engaged in fighting, or on his horse before the Battle of Maldon, encouraging the soldiers. A fragment of embroidery was discovered on the Oseberg Viking ship, showing a mounted horseman, horses pulling wagons, and foot-soldiers armed with shields and spears, the figures presented on different levels and all in strict profile, the whole remarkably like the design of the Aberlemno battle scene, though inferior in drawing. The Bayeux Tapestry is of course the greatest example of early secular tapestry. Its accomplish-ment suggests that it sprang from a long tradition. The scenes of horsemen and foot-soldiers at the beginning of the Battle of Hastings are strikingly similar to the Aberlemno battle scene, not simply because of the subject matter, but also because of the whole manner of the design.

It can be said that secular scenes, whether literary or historical, were presented in the Dark Age in the form of embroidery. Embroideries in fact alone offered scope for cycles of secular scenes, since manuscript illumination was geared to the require-ments of the clergy, who alone made use of books. Further, secular subject matter was naturally of more interest to the laity, whose dwellings woul' require hangings for their enhancement.

Since the Aberlemno battle scene is the type of subject nor-mally found at a later date in embroidery, we might tentatively

suggest that it is based on a native tapestry tradition no other
evidence for which has survived. If the front of the Aberlemno
Churchyard stone is to be read as a folio in stone, then the back
might be thought of as a stone cloth hanging.

No other Pictish sculptor attempted a battle scene of the Aberlemno type, but comparatively early in the history of Class II
the Pictish artists appear to have invented, or adopted from a
native source of the type discussed above, or for some foreign
type, a stereotyped hunting scene formula. This fixed type is
seen at its most effective, perhaps, on the Hilton of Cadboll
stone. Features of this design are the diagonal alignment of the
huntsmen and the placing, in the space thus left below the
leader, of a leaping hind being attacked simultaneously on the
shoulder and flank by two racing hounds. Although contained
in a small space, the design conveys astonishingly well the impression of fleeting movement. Once established, the hunt pattern was repeated with minor variations again and again. The
motif of the following trumpeters found on the Hilton of Cadboll stone is a later addition to the formula which will be discussed below.

A group of stones located in the south only can aptly be
described as 'monster stones'. These are Rossie, Dunfallandy,
St Vigeans (Romilly Allen's Nos. 1, 4), Gask, Woodwray,
Inchbrayock and a number of Meigle stones (Romilly Allen's
Nos. 4, 5, 9, 23).

The fantastic animals which appear on these stones when
reduced to their basic types are eight in number. They are not
simply fantastic lacertilians of the type common in contemporary manuscripts and metalwork, but are fully articulated, and
drawn with all the preoccupation with expressive detail that
characterizes the treatment of allegorical beasts. This fact, taken
with the limited number of types involved, strongly suggests
that certain workshops confined themselves to one specific literary source.

Plate 60

Plates 47–49,
53–55

Fig. 29

137

Joseph Anderson suggested that a version of the *Physiologus* lay behind this aspect of the animal iconography of Class II. The earliest extant illustrated *Physiologus* can be dated to the ninth century but it is perfectly possible that earlier illustrated versions existed.

A source even more promising than the *Physiologus*, one which Anderson does not mention, is the illustrated version of the *Marvels of the East*. The Anglo-Saxon version in British Museum, Cotton MS. Vitellius A.xv. contains a considerable number of motifs involving monstrous animals and monstrous men which bear a close resemblance to motifs on the Pictish stones. In his introduction to the Roxburghe Club facsimile, M.R. James makes the interesting suggestion that an illustrated version of the *Marvels* was part of the *Cosmographia* which Abbot Ceolfrith gave to King Aldfrith in exchange for a piece of land. Ceolfrith, as we have seen, was in touch with the Picts and it is possible, therefore, that Picts could have seen the manuscript. Certainly sketches from a rare manuscript source such as this would account well for this element in Pictish iconography.

Whether or not a convincing relationship between the Pictish monuments and the *Physiologus* and the *Marvels of the East* can be established, there is no doubt that the appearance of monstrous men and monstrous animals on Pictish stones is to be interpreted as reflecting the extraordinary interest in monster lore found throughout Europe in the eighth and ninth centuries.

The final element in the secular iconography of Class II is a *Fig. 30* miscellaneous group of figure scenes each of which appear on one stone only and which are difficult to identify. There are scenes involving a cauldron at Fowlis Wester, Glamis and Ulbster. All vary in composition. There is a preoccupation with beast-headed, and more particularly bird-men, as at Papil *Fig. 31* and Rossie. Representations of men knifing or wrestling with animals, again each with its own design, are numerous. This similarity of theme with variety of illustration may suggest that

Fig. 29. Fantastic animals, Class II: a, b, c. Rossie, Perthshire; d, e, f. Gask, Perthshire; g, k. Woodwray **Perthshire**; *h. Meigle 26, Perthshire; i, j. Meigle 23; l. Murthly, Perthshire*

we are dealing with individual representations of some legendary subject. They may, however, simply be variants of stock
motifs which have lost all meaning. The type of subject represented is found on contemporary continental metalwork such
as the well-known Burgundian buckles and Torslunda
plaques. A recurring Classical motif on the Pictish relief sculptures is the centaur, also found on Irish crosses, and there is a
single representation of what may be a Triton.

Fig. 32a, b

Fig. 30. Fantastic scenes, Class II: a. Murthly, Perthshire; b. Kettins, Angus; c. Meigle 26, Perthshire; d. Rossie, Perthshire; e. Woodwray, Perthshire

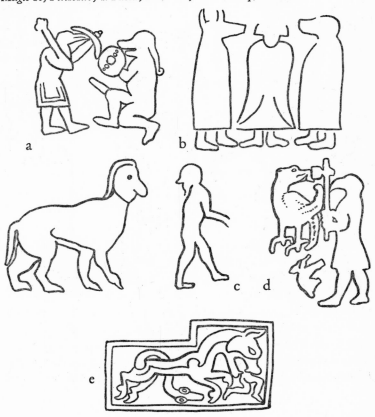

Fig. 31. St Vigeans 7, Angus, sacrifice of bull

ECLETICISM AND PICTISH ART

Before passing to a consideration of the Christian iconography of Class II it is necessary to draw attention to a distinctive characteristic of the Pictish artist's attitude to his secular motifs. The more Class II and Class III Pictish sculptures are studied the more apparent it becomes that the designers of these monuments worked on an entirely eclectic principle, filling in the areas not occupied by the cross with a haphazard array of motifs which have no cumulative significance; the exception to this

141

Fig. 32. Two Classical motifs: a. Centaur with foliated branches and axes, Aberlemno Roadside, Angus. b. Triton and two beasts, Meigle 22, Perthshire

Plate 57

being the never repeated, Aberlemno battle scene. The giant cross slab at Meigle imposes upon its motifs a unity of scale but makes no other link between them. The mounted men have nothing to do, iconographically speaking, with Daniel in the lions' den; Daniel has nothing to do with the centaur bearing the centaury plant; and the centaur has nothing to do with the climax of a hunting scene at the bottom of the slab. On other stones, motifs like beast-headed men fighting, or a man holding two birds by the neck, or fantastic beasts such as have been described above do not play a part in any meaningful programme of imagery, but are introduced for their own pictorial value and particularly for their usefulness as space-fillers.

142

This eclectic principle cannot readily be paralleled. There is nothing comparable in Dark Age sculpture in this country, and Ireland has at once fewer 'indifferent' motifs, and a much richer Christian iconography.

The haphazard picking-up of manifestly alien motifs is a characteristic of the workshop responsible for the great cauldron from Gundestrup, North Jutland. The cauldron also offers many specific parallels to the Pictish sculptures, some of which are well known; for example, the man held upside-down over a block or cauldron, and the man about to stab a bull. Many other examples could be cited. Motifs which are quite irrecon-

Fig. 33

cilable if they were intended to show forth a meaning, or to fall into a general context other than artistic, are lumped to-gether both in the cauldron and in Pictish sculptures. The mentality, and it seems some of the materials, of the first-century Gaulish metalworkers re-emerge, somehow or other, in Pictish Class II and III.

The eclectic mentality clearly survived for many centuries among Celtic metalworkers since it is fully apparent in the two

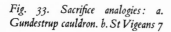

Fig. 33. Sacrifice analogies: a. Gundestrup cauldron. b. St Vigeans 7

a   b

Gallehus horns which are much closer to the Pictish sculptures in date than Gundestrup. These horns, also from Jutland, bear a great display of isolated motifs, many of which appear in Pictish sculpture. These motifs are scattered about the extensive surface of the horns with an obvious indifference to any specific iconographical content and with a full appreciation of their formal variety and vigour. This willingness to absorb motifs from all sorts of sources, and to re-employ them in a haphazard fashion would seem to confirm the suggestion that the artistic attitude of Class II–III Pictish sculptors was somehow formed in the atmosphere and environment of Dark Age continental Celtic metalwork.

The best-known example of artistic eclecticism in Dark Age art in Britain is, of course, the Franks Casket and it is interesting that there should be a stylistic link between this intensely eclectic production and Pictish art. The wolf and the horse definitely recall Pictish animal designs and many other parallels could be quoted. The eclecticism of the designer of the casket involved the juxtaposition of unified illustrations of totally diverse stories and traditions. Pictish artists made no such use of unified pictorial types, if indeed such things were even available to them. Pictish sculpture, it would seem, belongs to a more primitive artistic tradition than does the Franks Casket.

CHRISTIAN ICONOGRAPHY

Early Christian iconography concerns principally the Types of Salvation taken from the Old Testament and which are still found in the Prayers for the Dead. Only two of the Types occur in Pictish art, Daniel in the lions' den, and Jonah and the whale. These particular scenes are in fact the most common of the Types found in Early Christian art, their popularity perhaps owing something to their similarity to the folk motifs of the Hero's combat with an animal and the man-devouring monster.

There are only two Pictish stones which bear the Daniel motif and this leaves one quite unprepared for the magnificence of its rendering on one of the examples, the Meigle cross already referred to (page 142). Here Daniel is a hieratic figure, apparently bearded, with a long flaring robe. Four lions are disposed around his outstretched arms, and two smaller animals placed above the upper lions may also belong to the composition. A forepaw of each of the four large lions touches the Prophet. The heavy heads and their general plasticity are Classical in mood but the carefully arranged tails and high groins taken with the presence of the Daniel figure suggest a Byzantine source.

Plate 57

The Meigle Daniel is most closely paralleled on the market-place cross at Kells in Ireland, which belongs most probably to the tenth century. Irish sculptors appear to have had access to a number of Daniel types and it seems probable that the Pictish sculptor of the Meigle stone has produced the most impressive version of a Daniel type known in Ireland.

There are only two scenes on Pictish cross slabs which can with reasonable certainty be identified as Jonah and the whale. The earliest is at Fowlis Wester, where at the top right of the slab a nude Jonah lies beside a simplified dog-headed sea-monster. The later version at Dunfallandy could have been taken directly from an Early Christian sarcophagus; the wolf-head, the large fin and the U-bend on the whale's fat tail are entirely typical. The Fowlis Wester nude may also be compared with the figure of Jonah reclining under the gourd on Christian sarcophagi. There are no comparable treatments of this subject in Irish art.

Plate 43

On the reverse of the late Inchbrayock slab a warrior is shown striking a cleric on the head with a peculiar implement, probably intended for an animal's jaw-bone. The hooked ramus and large ridged teeth are clearly enough rendered, but most oddly the teeth have been wrongly placed in the underpart of the jaw.

Fig. 34a

Two characters in art use a jaw-bone as a weapon, namely Samson and Cain. One is tempted to see in the Inchbrayock slab a representation of Cain murdering Abel, since the contrast between the costume of the warrior and his victim agrees with a later medieval habit of making clear pictorial distinction between the dress and general appearance of the virtuous Abel and the wicked Cain.

The earliest certain representation of Cain armed with a jaw-bone is in an Anglo-Saxon manuscript produced at Canterbury shortly before the Norman Conquest, but a tenth-century cross at Monasterboice in Ireland may perhaps show Cain with a jaw-bone. If the Inchbrayock warrior is Cain, he provides a notably early example of this particular iconography.

On the whole, however, Samson seems the more likely candidate. One can imagine that the ultimate source of the Pictish carving would be a book illustration like the fine one in the ninth-century Homilies of St Gregory Nazianzen in Paris, where Samson vigorously wields the jaw-bone, to smite a Philistine fallen at his feet.

Fig. 34b

That Samson is the subject of the carving, and that a distinguished model lies behind the Pictish version, is perhaps confirmed by a feature of the right-hand group on the front of the slab. Mrs Curle has identified this group as Delilah cutting off Samson's hair, but has not analyzed the composition in detail. Now we may notice that the small figure at the left has a very long arm, bent at the elbow. The forearm runs up vertically towards the terminal of the lock of hair which descends from the top of the figure's head. This lock of hair is of the same thickness as his arm. It is possible that in the model on which these figures ultimately depend, the lock of hair was in fact the left arm of Samson; that is, Samson's arms were placed in such a position that he could rest his head upon them. Precisely this is the position of Samson in the scene of Delilah's treachery in the Greek Homilies, and in a later copy of the Homilies picture

Fig. 34. Samson imagery: a. Samson killing the Philistines, Inchbrayock, Perthshire. b. Samson betrayed by Delilah, Inchbrayock, Perthshire. c. Delilah cutting off Samson's hair. Illustration of Book of Judges *from the* Arsenal Bible, Paris

in the thirteenth-century Arsenal Bible. In the Homilies and the Arsenal Bible Samson lies asleep with his head and arms supported on Delilah's knees. As a result his head is on a level with her waist. This difference in head level is maintained in the Pictish sculpture, but because the complex reclining posi- tion of Samson was too much for him, the incompetent copyist has turned Samson into a dwarf. Despite the poorness of his work, however, he has left important clues as to the design of his model, which would appear to have been akin to very important Greek representations of Samson.

Fig. 34c

Pictish sculptors had access to a series of illustrations con- cerning incidents in the lives of Saint Paul and Saint Anthony. In an age of monasticism it is not difficult to account for the veneration of these two saints – Saint Paul, the first hermit, and St Anthony, the great patriarch of monks. Their *Lives*, written respectively by St Jerome and St Athanasius, must have been well known and the interest taken in these two hermit-saints at this period is attested by the depiction of incidents from their lives on Irish, Northumbrian and Pictish Dark Age sculptures.

The Pictish sculptors portrayed three illustrations on this theme. The first shows a formal arrangement of the two saints

Fig. 35

on either side of the cross with seemingly determinative symbols placed above them rather in the manner of the portrayal of the Evangelists. The symbol for St Paul is his date-palm which provided him with food and clothing, and for St Anthony a figure representing the Heavenly Vision which appeared to him at his time of greatest molestation by demons. This scene is shown on a stone at Fowlis Wester and appears in a truncated version at Dunfallandy.

Plate 44

The second scene illustrates the famous incident told by Jerome of how the raven which usually provided Paul with half a loaf of bread, brought a whole loaf when St Anthony was visiting him. Jerome tells how there was a contention between them as to which of them should break the loaf, and how this was resolved by each of them holding on to it and pulling. This incident is shown on St Vigeans (Romilly Allen's No. 7), where the saints are seated, both holding the bread. A line drawn through the loaf indicates that the bread is about to break but the raven (now mutilated, but visible) holds it in his beak, providing a neat conflation of the sequence of events.

Plate 45

On the Nigg pediment the scene represented would seem to be prior to the division of the bread. The raven descends with the whole loaf and the saints kneel under the date-palm in thanksgiving for the miracle. The raven places the loaf on a paten, for here, as in certain Irish treatments of the subject, the bread and its subsequent breaking is thought-of in terms of the Mass. The dog-like creatures at either side of the paten are presumably the two lions which helped St Anthony to bury St Paul.

Plate 61

It is unlikely that the Picts had access to illustrations of St Paul and St Anthony which were not available to Irish and Northumbrian sculptors, and we can suppose that their fuller treatment is due to the larger areas which they had to cover, together with their general interest in the portrayal of figure scenes.

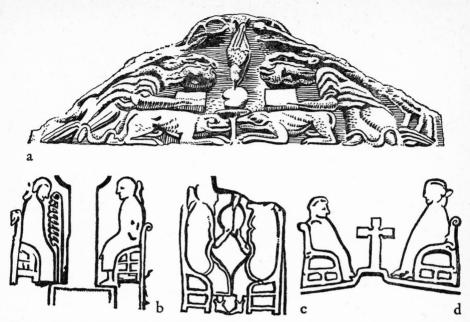

Fig. 35. Meeting of SS. Anthony and Paul: a. Nigg, Ross-shire. b. Fowlis Wester, Perthshire. c. St Vigeans 7, Angus. d. Dunfallandy, Perthshire

In this review of the Christian iconography depicted on the Class II and Class III monuments I have left until last a discussion of the highly interesting and important David iconography that appears on a most important group of related monuments which have already received some attention, namely, the St Andrews Sarcophagus and the slabs at Nigg and Aber‑lemno Roadside. Plates 59, 61, 62 These, and minor related monuments were clearly produced under the inspiration of new influences which can best be defined by a simultaneous discussion of their style and iconography.

The St Andrews Sarcophagus must be regarded as the most ambitious of the various, historically connected, attempts to re‑construct the sarcophagus shape, such as the early Mercian coped tombstone at Wirksworth, Derbyshire, the Jedburgh shrine and the St Leonard's School shrine. (The tradition of small carved boxes now solely represented by the Franks Casket is probably also of relevance in this connection.)

The design of the different sections of the St Andrews Sarcophagus suggests that it is an original native effort made to conform with a general notion, but nothing more, of an antique sarcophagus. It is, as it were, a box made out of parts of an upright cross slab. The framed and self-contained figure scene can be compared with the framed figure scene on the cross slab at Hilton of Cadboll. The essential feature of a cross slab, the cross itself, appears on the end of the sarcophagus. In the decoration of the recumbent slabs at Meigle the response of the sculptors to this new shape of monument is exactly the same. Familiar elements from the upright cross slab are merely imposed upon the new shape.

Hitherto the source of the figure panel has been supposed to have been a portable object, that is, an ivory carving, of a distinctly Orientalizing tendency. Among her evidence for this Oriental quality of the archetype, Mrs Curle quotes the 'Assyrian' lions and the animals entangled in a tree. The St Andrews lions, it is true, differ from the dog-like lion of the Book of Durrow and the stolid naturalistic lion in the St Mark page of the Lindisfarne Gospels, but they do not represent a novel and unprecedented type. They are the rampant snarling short-faced lions of the St Mark pages in the Lichfield and Echternach Gospels. That is, they are of a type recognized in Hiberno-Saxon manuscript painting from the very start.

Mrs Curle illustrates a panel from a Coptic chest as an analogy for the tree among whose branches the St Andrews animals run. As good an analogy can be found much nearer home. On the Franks Casket two men armed with spears enter a thicket in pursuit of the wolf, which they then observe suckling Romulus and Remus. The running wolf is inserted into the tree exactly

Plate 64

Plate 46

Fig. 36

Plate 51

Fig. 36. Lichfield Gospels, Lion of St Mark

as the deer is inserted in the sarcophagus tree. The three leaf
terminals of the sarcophagus tree correspond well with groups
of three leaves on the Franks Casket tree. Against the body of
the rampant lion and also in the extreme left-hand top corner
of the panel the branches of the sarcophagus tree are interwoven
into a symmetrical pattern. This formal arrangement of leafy
branches is paralleled again in the Lichfield Gospels, in the
branch held by St Luke and also in the panel of symmetrical
foliage growing from a main stem at Fletton, one of the two
principal monuments of Mercian sculpture. The delicately
drawn St Andrews animals passing among slender branches
are remarkably akin in spirit to the gay Mercian animals entangled among branches at both Fletton and Breedon, and the
little cat-like lions with almost human faces at Breedon offer
the best parallel for the squatting creature immediately to the
left of the rampant lion in the sarcophagus, and also for the apes
on the end panel.

Plate 64

It would be as well, therefore, to withdraw the St Andrews
Sarcophagus from any ill-defined Northumbrian context, and
to associate it fully with the artistic developments centred on
Mercia in the last quarter of the eighth century. The peculiar
zig-zag drapery of the St Andrews David can be closely paralleled in the fragmentary figure on the Reculver cross shaft

which represents English response to Carolingian influence in the period of Mercian domination. The most striking analogy for the figure of David, with the great flap of drapery over his arm, the fully plastic parallel fold and the thick tossing hem-line, is the angel bestowing the Greek blessing at Breedon. Apart from the drapery, the general proportions, the full-fleshed face, the heavy locks of hair, and the fat, strong hands of this angel agree very well with the St Andrews David.

Fig. 37

These stylistic parallels become all the more significant when we consider the important problem of David iconography find-ing its way into the Pictish area. In discussing David icono-graphy, Mrs Curle refers to primitive Early Christian David scenes and to highly developed Byzantine products such as the Cyprus silver dishes. No convincing link-up between these eastern David cycles and Pictland is attempted. However, David iconography makes its first appearance in Britain in the Durham Cassiodorus, with the separate figures of the seated psalmist and the standing warrior armed with a spear and disk, and then expands rapidly in the Canterbury Psalter, Cotton MS. Ves-pasian A.i, which is stylistically close to the Breedon angel and must be regarded as a characteristic product of Mercian culture, whether it was illustrated at Canterbury or Lichfield. The figure of David playing the harp in a full-page illustration agrees ad-mirably in its full plastic awareness, its zig-zag and pleated drapery, its classical feeling and its naturalism, with the St An-drews David. The first image of David rending the lion's jaws in insular art appears in the Canterbury Psalter, and though the lion is not rampant, David is standing erect as at St An-drews, not kneeling on the lion's back as in Byzantine versions.

David iconography appears to have moved northwards from St Andrews. A fragment survives at Elgin, but the major extant monument in this connection is at Nigg. The Nigg stone has two additional David images, the harp and the man with the cymbals, both to be deduced from Psalm 150. This northern

Fig. 37. David imagery: a. St Andrews, Fife. b. Elgin, Morayshire. c. Aberlemno Roadside, Angus. d. Nigg, Ross-shire. e. Aldbar, Angus. f. Dupplin, Perthshire

interest in David as musician may justify the suggestion that the Hilton of Cadboll sculptor makes eclectic use of David iconography in his version of the hunting scene. This contains the curious feature of the two trumpeters on foot at the top right-hand corner. They are placed in depth, one beyond the other. In the full-page miniature in the Canterbury Psalter, David is surrounded by dancers and musicians. At the bottom left and right are a pair of musicians, set in depth one beyond the other, lifting up and blowing trumpets. These trumpeters offer a good parallel for the Hilton of Cadboll trumpeters, and have the important merit of being found in insular art at about the right time. This gives them an advantage over analogies from Persian rock carvings mentioned by Mrs Curle. For the figure of the woman rider, however, the Gaulish Epona type provides perhaps the most striking parallel, as does the Hippolytus hunting, on a south French Roman sarcophagus for the hunting scene.

Fig. 38

Common allegiance to Mercian artistic developments ties together the St Andrews Sarcophagus, the cross slab at Nigg, and the cross slab at Hilton of Cadboll. The stem of the cross at Nigg, and the crescent symbol at Hilton of Cadboll are decorated with the key pattern which is one of the characteristics of Mercian manuscript decoration. Similarly the loose all-over pattern of trumpet spirals below the hunting scene at Hilton of Cadboll is Mercian-inspired. Compare it, for example, with a panel at South Kyme. The attenuated birds in the broad side bands at Hilton of Cadboll have much in common with the birds on the Mercian Ormside Bowl but are virtually identical to the birds pecking vines in the Rome Gospels, which is Mercian work of about 800.

Plates 60, 61

The Hilton of Cadboll trumpeters are portrayed in depth. In the version of this motif on Aberlemno Roadside the trumpeters are moved into the same plane, one following the other. This arrangement must be regarded as a debasement, and the Hilton of Cadboll version must therefore have priority over the south-

Plates 59, 60

Fig. 38. Hilton of Cadboll, Ross-shire, comparisons: a. Hilton of Cadboll, woman riding. b. Epona from Gaulish Celtic stele from Agassac (after Pobé). c. Hilton of Cadboll, trumpeters. d. David's musicians from the Canterbury Psalter. e. Hilton of Cadboll, hunting scene. f. Hippolytus hunting, from sarcophagus, Lapidarium, Arles (after Pobé)

ern version. At Aberlemno the scene of the huntsmen and trumpeters is associated within the hunting scene with the walk' ing figure (of David?) from the St Andrews Sarcophagus and Nigg, and outside the hunting scene proper with a figure of David rending the lion's jaws. This is interesting, if the sug' gestion that the Hilton of Cadboll trumpeters are ultimately connected with the Mercian musicians of David is acceptable.

The most northern phase of Mercian artistic influence is found in the Book of Kells. Kells was deeply influenced by Carolingian art, notably in the design of the canon tables, and in the extensive and novel New Testament iconography. In the British Isles Canterbury in the South and Lichfield in the Midlands were the great reception centres for Carolingian in' fluence. That influence will have reached the North by way of Mercia, and in terms of Mercian artistic style. The figure style in the Book of Kells has to be understood in the light of Mercian sculpture, notably the Breedon figures. The cumbrous propor' tions, the sense of plasticity, the thick fleshy drapery, and above all the latent emotionalism exhibited in the blessing angel and the bust'length virgin at Breedon, reappear only slightly exag' gerated in the great New Testament figures in Kells.

Since Kells is to such a large extent merely the latest phase in the reception of Mercian influences in the North, it is natural that the group of related monuments under discussion should exhibit features definitely belonging to the Kells school. The cross slab at Nigg contains a rather debased version of the St Andrews David scene, and should therefore be later than the St Andrew's Sarcophagus. The St Paul and St Anthony group, the iconography of which was discussed above, is de' signed very much in the figure style of Kells. The snakes and bosses of Nigg we have seen to be paralleled in a gilt bronze object of Irish origin. In this piece of metalwork three of the curved thick'bodied snakes terminate in large staring human faces. This is precisely a feature of the *XPI* page of Kells, so that the snakes and bosses of the bronze object and of the Nigg stone have to be understood as the expression in cast and carved sculpture of the artistic ideas of the Kells school.

The last monument of this group is Aberlemno Roadside, in which the Hilton of Cadboll figure scene is reproduced in association with the St Andrews David scene as interpreted at Nigg. At Aberlemno Roadside mourning angels are placed at either side of the cross. This is an emotional extension of the meaning of the interlace cross unprecedented in insular art. From being a triumphal motif, essentially abstract in form but related in significance to the figures of Christ-as-Victor on the Ruthwell and Bewcastle crosses, the interlace cross is now endowed with the significance of a crucifix. This remarkable iconographical advance must be due to Carolingian influence. We can compare the hunched and stooping posture of the Aberlemno angels with angels adoring and sympathizing with the figure of Christ on the cross in Metz-school ivories. The school of Kells provides the only possible background for the remarkable Aberlemno angels. Kells was in touch with Carol-ingian ideas, was up-to-date iconographically, and tends to-wards a rather heady emotionalism in its designs.

Plate 58

From the above analyses of the Pictish sculptural style and iconography, it will be seen that in the present writer's opinion Pictish sculpture in no way represents a late or provincial reflec-tion of the main developments in Hiberno-Saxon art; it was, rather, the creation of artists freely participating in the evolution of that style and contributing to it some of its most daring and magnificent monuments.

THE MEANING OF THE SYMBOLS

Before bringing to a close this survey of Pictish art it is only fair to raise, at least briefly, the difficult question of the possible meaning of the symbols on the stones. It is frustrating not to know what this well-attested series of designs, in use right through the historical period, means. Without wishing to appear defeatist, it cannot be said that the prospects of understanding the symbolism in detail are very great, short of the unlikely discovery of a contemporary literary reference or of a sculpture itself depicting clear equivalents. It is tantalizing to realize that Adomnan must have known, at least in general, what the Pictish symbols conveyed, but this is only one of the many omissions by that writer which the student of the Picts has reason to lament.

The evidence for tattooing among the Picts has been discussed in an earlier chapter (page 33). Some writers have suggested that the 'likenesses of animals' and 'all sorts of drawings' described by Herodian as decorating the bodies of the Picts are in fact our symbol designs, and further, that the assertion in Isidore of Seville that these signs conveyed the personal rank of the individual provides the answer to the problem of their meaning. The fact remains that while a connection between the tattoo designs and the symbols is an interesting suggestion, the connection between these late Classical references and the stones as we know them can never be proved. The tattoo designs may have been very different in appearance. Moreover, the suggestion has the weakness that doubt has been cast on the validity of the tradition which lies behind the references themselves. The suggestion, of course, can be made; but to pursue it at any length is not profitable, for at the base of the arguments lies an undemonstrable fact. The only valid basis for a discussion of the meaning of the symbols must be in terms of the symbols as we actually know them, that is, on the stones and other related artifacts. In this connection a few brief points can be made.

It is most unlikely that the symbols convey Christian concepts, as has sometimes been thought. The symbols carried a meaning independent of the cross but the meaning caused no offence to the cross, and indeed there was some common relevance shared by the symbols and the cross which made it apt for them to appear together. Otherwise the Picts could easily have had two independent series of monuments, cross slabs and symbol stones.

The silver jewellery and the stones with inscriptions contain, ing personal names suggest that the symbols had a personal application. They are less likely to be such things as stones marking the sites of famous battles, or boundary stones. In con, nection with the silver chains it is perhaps worth noting that, according to a medieval source, prior to the death of Rhodri Mawr (died 877) the Welsh kings did not wear crowns but instead had gold chains. The word used is 'hual', which has the meaning 'a fetter, gyve or shackle', a description which fits the massive Pictish silver chains well. However, to attribute characteristics of Welsh society to the Picts is no more justifi, able than it is to attribute features of Irish society to them.

Plate 18

It has yet to be proved that the stones were regularly used as headstones. A few burials have been found in apparent associ, ation with symbol-bearing stones but other examples which have had the surrounding ground carefully explored have shown no such connection.

Tattooing apart, the personal rank or profession interpretation is the one most commonly found in the literature on the sub, ject. But it has to accommodate such difficulties as the apparent extraordinary versatility of the Picts. Surely some of the Picts were memorable by virtue of some single personal quality or achievement. We certainly have no evidence for different classes of society among the Picts to whom the various symbols could be assigned. The King and Sub-King formulation, however apt ethnologically, is based solely on a twelfth-century source which, in the present writer's opinion at least, has been over, valued. The only Pictish official title mentioned in the early written sources are the royal 'exactatores' who died fighting alongside Nechton in 728.

Perhaps the most remarkable of the many remarkable aspects of these monuments is the sheer number of them – and there may once have been many more. Whatever their meaning, they clearly refer to an important if relatively common aspect of day-to-day Pictish living or dying.

There is much to commend the view that, whatever their particular meaning, towards the end of the series the symbols came to be thought of as a national flag. The large prominently displayed symbols on such stones as Aberlemno Roadside, Rosemarkie Churchyard, and the Maiden Stone, would certainly bear out this interpretation. The disappearance of the symbols in Class III would then tell its own story.

Plate 65

Note on the Historical Sources

Undoubtedly the air of mystery which surrounds the Picts is due to a large extent to the lack of native sources. A people without written records at once suggests illiteracy and general cultural backwardness. Why are the native sources represented only by a king list?

We can, I think, safely dismiss the suggestion that no written records were, in fact, kept by the Picts. There is nothing in the contemporary foreign sources to suggest that the Picts did not have normal monastic scriptoria or that records were not kept there. In Bede's *Ecclesiastical History*, for example, there is a specific reference to Easter Tables being *transcribed* in the monasteries of the Picts.

There are two forms in which Pictish sources could have survived. The manuscripts of the records themselves dating to AD 850 and earlier, could have been preserved. Manuscripts as early as this containing important source material for early Irish and English history do exist, but the great majority of the contemporary sources for the history of these countries are to be found in manuscripts of a much later period. The lack of even one contemporary Pictish manuscript, while still remarkably unfortunate, is therefore not altogether surprising.

What *is* surprising is why native sources have not come down to us in this second form – as transcriptions in later manuscripts. The question to be answered, therefore, is not so much why there are no native contemporary sources for the history of the Picts, as why Pictish sources were not transcribed at a later period.

There is no doubt that the disappearance of Pictish as an official language under the Scottish régime must account for the loss of certain sources. As time passed, vernacular Pictish sources would become incomprehensible and the likelihood of their being transcribed very remote. This would not account, however, for the failure of Latin Pictish sources to be transcribed. Moreover, there must have been at least a certain amount of administrative continuity in ecclesiastical and secular affairs at the time of the changeover from the Pictish to a Scottish supremacy, and the lack of Pictish sources cannot be satisfactorily explained by the unwarranted hypothesis of the sudden disappearance of all things Pictish after the accession of Kenneth. What we should expect to find is transcriptions of Gaelicized versions of Pictish material and this we do in the case of one version of the king list. Certainly there would be a tendency for some types of material to be allowed to disappear after the introduction of a Scottish administration – Pictish laws for example. The collections of Anglo-Saxon laws owe their survival to a sudden interest in Anglo-Saxon law in the twelfth century. Only a comparable interest in Pictish affairs on the part of Scots of later periods could have led to the survival of this type of material. In later periods the history of the Picts seems to have been of interest only in so far as, by manipulation, it could be used to extend the antiquity of the Scottish line. For such a purpose a king list was of particular use and this may account for the survival of this particular native source.

What kinds of records did the new Scottish administration keep? It is here that we are brought to the heart of the problem, for the supply of native source material for the two hundred years after 850 is just as deficient as it is for the 550–850 period. In other words the lack of native Pictish sources is part of the larger problem of the lack of Scottish sources for up until about 1070 – the time of Queen Margaret. There can be no doubt at all that written records were kept for this later period, but for some reason they too failed to be transcribed sufficiently often for them to have survived. The exact reasons for this cannot be discussed here, but the Danish raids of the ninth and early tenth centuries, the depredations of Edward I in the thirteenth century and the destruction of cathedral archives at the time of the Reformation must all have contributed to the loss of such transcriptions of early material as there were. What is important in this connection is that it should be recognized that the lack of native source material has nothing to do with the cultural and intellectual achievement of the Picts.

The two most important sources for the history of the Picts are the lists of the Pictish kings and the Pictish material in the collections of Irish *Annals*. A brief account of the nature of these sources follows.

THE LISTS OF THE KINGS

Fig. 39   Eight principal versions of the list of the Pictish succession of kings and their reign lengths have survived. These eight lists represent versions of

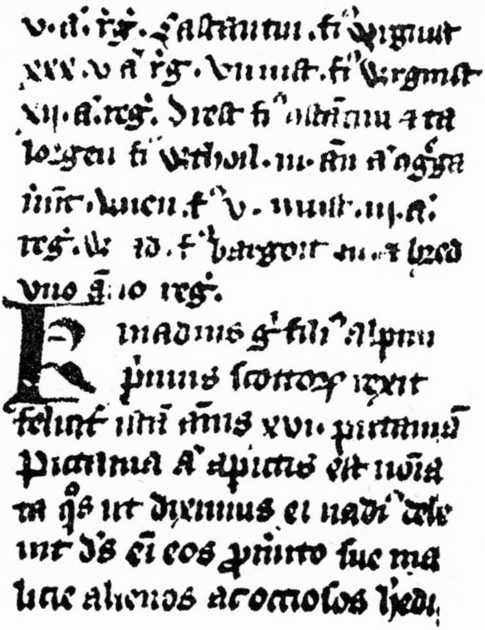

Fig. 39. Section of the most authoritative list of the Pictish kings showing the end of the Pictish and the beginning of the Scottish succession. Fol. 28vo, Paris, Bib. Nat., Lat. 4126

two basic texts which for convenience are known as List 1 and List 2. The best text of List 1 is in a fourteenth-century manuscript Bib. Nat. Latin MS. 4126. This is a historical miscellany which contains other Scottish materials including the topographical surveys known as the *De Situ Albanie*. It has been suggested that these Scottish items were materials for a history of Scotland collected by a twelfth-century author. The list is attached to a chronicle of events during the reigns of the early Scottish kings, referred to in this book as the Scottish Chronicle. This chronicle was probably compiled in the tenth century and if the Pictish list was attached to it, then – and this has been disputed – we have a terminus date for it also. This is the most important version of all because it preserves the kings' names in, as far as one can tell, their Pictish forms.

There is no best version for List 2, for all of them are very late and corrupt. In the basic text of this list the kings' names have been Gaelicized by a transcriber.

List 1 has about forty names at the beginning not found in List 2. They are the eponymous Cruithne and his seven sons, seven other names taken apparently from an Irish source, and a list of thirty kings all of whom are called *Brude*. Thereafter List 1 and List 2 contain approximately the same material.

There has been some controversy concerning the relationship between the two basic texts. W. F. Skene thought that they shared a common written archetype and that any discrepancies were due to the insertion of local kings in one of the lists. Professor H. M. Chadwick, on the other hand, thought that they were compiled independently from oral tradition current in different parts of the country. Mrs M. O. Anderson, the authority on the lists, suggests that they are dependent on the same archetype up to the reign of Nechton, son of Derile (706–724), but that thereafter they are independent.

This is not a suitable place to present detailed arguments, but I believe that a common written source lies behind the first twenty-one names shared by the lists, for there the differences between the two texts can be almost wholly accounted for in terms of scribal corruption of a common text. On the other hand, the differences in the later part of the lists, which includes all the historical kings, can, I think, best be explained by supposing the two lists to have been independently derived from the same set of annals. The reasons for believing this can be briefly stated as follows. First, none of the divergences between the lists can be explained in terms of scribal errors of transcription. Secondly, the reign-length discrepancies are not of the type due to the misreading of Roman numerals, but are in terms of a year or two. They look, therefore, like errors of calculation. Thirdly, the period of acute divergence in the eighth-century succession could well be the result of the interpretation of an annalistic record of what was in fact a period of great political confusion. Beyond this period the comparative agreement between the two lists is resumed.

These hypothetical annals used by the compilers of the lists are unlikely to have been Irish, for the kings' names were available in their Pictish forms. They could have been British or Northumbrian, for Pictish name forms are retained in these foreign sources. The likelihood, however, of a foreign scriptorium keeping a complete record of the Pictish succession is somewhat remote. There remains the interesting possibility that they were Pictish. A possible context for the compilation might be very tentatively proposed as the reign of Nechton, son of Derilei. It was under this king's authority that the 84-year-cycle Easter Tables were destroyed and the 19-year cycle substituted. It was common practice to annotate Easter Tables with brief notices concerning such events as the death of an abbot or king, so that this information could have been brought together after the cycle itself had been abandoned.

By the end of the seventh century some kind of chronicle was being kept in Northumbria and it was under Northumbrian influence that Nechton had brought about the change in the calculation of Easter. He also em-barked on the building of a stone church in Pictland under the super-vision of Northumbrian architects. The extraction of the notes from the margins of the old Easter Tables and their use in the compilation of a chronicle could be another manifestation of Nechton's desire to emulate Northumbrian culture.

THE IRISH ANNAL COLLECTIONS

The most important collections of Irish annals for the history of the Picts are the *Annals of Tigernach* (Bodleian MS. Rawl. B 488) and the *Annals of Ulster* (Trinity College Dublin MS. H.1.8.).

Fig. 40

Irish scholars are agreed that behind all the major collections of annals there lies an original Old-Irish chronicle which began at the Patrician period. The exact date of the compilation of this original chronicle is a matter of debate, Professor Mac Neill favouring the beginning, and Pro-fessor O'Rahilly the middle, of the eighth century.

It is highly probable that among the materials used by the compiler of the original chronicle there was a record which had been kept on Iona, and that this record contained the majority of the references to Pictish affairs that are now to be found in the Irish *Annals*. The arguments for the existence of an Iona record have been based on a number of entries concerning the affairs of the community which appear to have been written on Iona. For example, in 676 Failbe, abbot of Iona, is said to have 'returned' from Ireland. The precise dating of some of the Iona entries would also seem to reflect the interest of the community itself. On the further question as to whether the Pictish material in the annals comes from the Iona record, two points have been made. First, the earliest of the very full sequence of the obits of Pictish kings to be recorded is that of

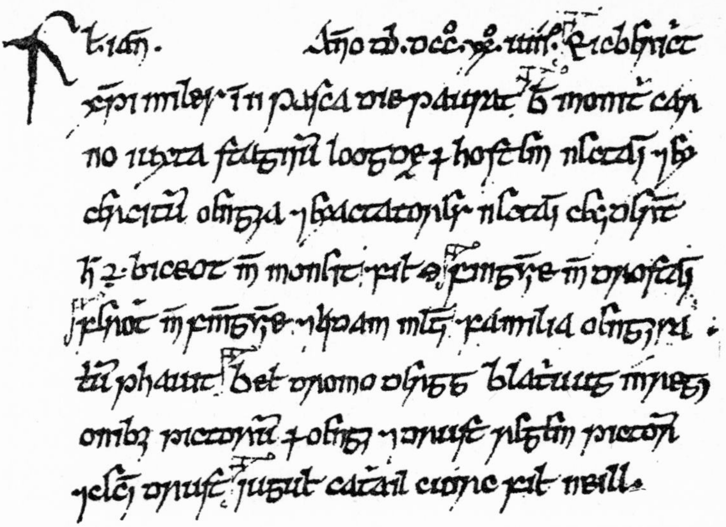

Fig. 40. Part of the Annals of Ulster, fol. 28ᵛᵒ, T.C.D., MS. H. 1. 8., showing the year section for AD 728 (recte 729)

Bridei, son of Maelcon, in whose reign Iona was founded. Secondly, in year sections where there are entries concerning Iona, Pictland and Dalriada, the entries are grouped together and are very often found in an initial position.

The number of entries in the annals for Iona in the pre-750 period is in itself a powerful argument for the use by the compiler of an Iona record. Only two other monastic centres have a comparable series of entries – Clonmacnoise and Bangor. There is, moreover, as one would expect if an Iona record was being used, a marked change in the nature of the Iona entries for the period after 750 when the annals were being kept contemporaneously. The marked contrast in the entries at almost exactly 750 lends powerful support to Professor O'Rahilly's date for the compilation of the original chronicle. After this date the Iona abbot obits which had regularly held the initial position in their year section are now medially placed and, while the entries for the pre-750 period showed clear signs of having been written on Iona, the entries after 750 show equally clear signs of having been written in Ireland.

Further points in support of the view that the Pictish material came from this Iona record can also be made. There is no indication that a Pictish record was being used. The obits of the kings are recorded in such a variety of ways that the simple insertion of a king list could not account for them. Nor is there any sign of a pro-Pictish bias. For example, where Picts are fighting the Scots of Dalriada the interest of the recorder is never with the Picts but always with the Scots. If the Scots are defeated, the names of their slain are given, not the name of the Pictish victor.

On the other hand, the obits of the Pictish kings are recorded with great fidelity. There is an obit for every king in List 1 and all but one in List 2 from Cennalath to Nechton, son of Derilei. It is improbable that any insular Irish scriptorium would have kept such a full record of the deaths of the Pictish kings. It is even improbable that a Dalriadic scriptorium should do so. Only the position of Iona as head of the Church in Pictland can account for a non-Pictish source being sufficiently interested in the Pictish succession.

The Pictish entries are brief and have been made in a scriptorium where no identification or explanation of Pictish personalities and events are felt to be necessary. This intimate nature of the record, taken with the detached method of recording purely Pictish events and evident Dalriadic bias in others, can best be explained by their having been written on Iona.

One curious feature of the Pictish material in the Irish *Annals* requiring explanation is the fact that while the entries concerning Dalriada, which can also be shown to have been in the Iona record, virtually cease at 750 when that record dropped out of use, the Pictish entries pause for a decade but then start up again to come to an end about 840. It is very difficult indeed to suggest a source for these entries in any way compatible with the neglect of Dalriadic affairs. An insertion into a continuation of the original chronicle from a Pictish record seems to be the only explanation possible. A similar insertion of yet another record may account for the Dalriadic and Pictish entries which appear to be unique to the *Annals of Ulster,* although it is possible that these entries have for some reason been omitted from the other collections. When brought together this unique material has a definite western bias and it starts abruptly at about 670. It is possible that an annotated Easter Table from Applecross is the source involved.

Applecross was founded in 672 from the parent house of Bangor in Ireland, the monastic centre where, it has been suggested, the original chronicle may have been compiled.

The only remaining feature of the Pictish material which calls for comment is the series of entries describing the battles in the Pictish civil war of *c.* 730. These battles are very fully reported in the annals but the accounts in the *Annals of Tigernach* and the *Annals of Ulster* vary in detail and it looks as if these entries had stood in an even longer form in the original chronicle. Some kind of extended narrative source for the career of Oengus, son of Fergus, the principal contender for the throne, may, therefore, have been in the hands of the compiler.

This condensed account of the two most important sources for the history of the Picts may have served to illustrate some of the problems attached to their use. The Iona record probably did not amount to more than an annotated Easter Table. All the entries are in Latin and they are extremely brief. They are not the notices of a chronicler eager to record for posterity what seemed to him the historically significant aspects of important occasions. The entries read as mere diary notes recording in the main such facts as arrivals and departures of abbots and the travels of relics and their safe return, for the private convenience of the community. On the other hand, the entries from about 712 onwards do seem to be more ambitious; this perhaps reflects the change in the type of Easter Table which took place on Iona in 716.

We have seen also that within these sources there may be evidence for the existence of the native Pictish records that must have existed but which, so far at least, have not been discovered among the manuscript materials for the history of Scotland.

Select Bibliography

Abbreviations

A.J.	*Archaeological Journal*
P.P.	*The Problem of the Picts,* ed. F. T. Wainwright, Edinburgh, 1955.
P.P.S.	*Proceedings of the Prehistoric Society*
P.S.A.S.	*Proceedings of the Society of Antiquaries of Scotland*
S.G.S.	*Scottish Gaelic Studies*
S.H.R.	*Scottish Historical Review*

CHAPTER I

CHADWICK, N. K. 'Pictish and Celtic Marriage in Early Literary Tradition', *S.G.S.* VIII Pt ii (1958), 56–155.

— 'The Name Pict', *ibid.* 146–176.

CHILDE, V. G. 'The Experimental Production of the Phenomena Distinctive of Vitrified Forts', *P.S.A.S.* LXXII (1937–38), 44–55.

CHRISTISON, D. *Early Fortifications in Scotland,* Edinburgh, 1898.

COLLINGWOOD, R. G. and MYRES, J. N. L. *Roman Britain and the English Settlements,* Oxford, 2nd ed., 1937.

COTTON, M. AYLWIN. 'British Camps with Timber-laced Ramparts' *A.J.,* CXI (1954) 26–105.

CRAW, J. H. 'Excavations at Dunadd ...' *P.S.A.S.* LXIV (1929–30), 111–127.

FEACHEM, R. W. 'Fortifications' in *P.P.*

FRASER, J. 'The Question of the Picts' *S.G.S.* II (1927), 172–201.

GRAHAM, A. 'Some Observations on the Brochs', *P.S.A.S.* LXXXI (1946–47), 48–99.

— 'Archaeological Gleanings from Dark-Age Records', *P.S.A.S.* LXXXV (1950–51), 64–91.

HAMILTON, J. R. C. *Excavations at Jarlshof, Shetland,* Edinburgh, 1956.

— 'Brochs and Broch Builders', in *The Northern Isles,* ed. F. T. Wainwright, Edinburgh, 1962.

JACKSON, K. H. 'Two Early Scottish Names', *S.H.R.* XXXIII (1954), 14–18.

— 'The Pictish Language', *P.P.*

MacKIE, E. W. 'The Origin and Development of the Broch and Wheel-house Building Cultures of the Scottish Iron Age', *P.P.S.,* XXXI (1965), 93–146.

PIGGOTT, S. (ed.) *The Prehistoric Peoples of Scotland,* London, 1962.

— 'The Archaeological Background' in *P.P.*

RICHMOND, I. (ed.) *Roman and Native in North Britain,* Edinburgh, 1958.

O'RAHILLY, T. F. *Early Irish History and Mythology,* Dublin, 1946.

RIVET, A. L. F. 'The Iron Age in North Britain', *Antiquity* XXXVI (1962), 24–31.

SCOTT, W. L. 'The Problem of the Brochs', *P.P.S.,* XIII (1947), 1–36.

— 'Gallo-British Colonies. The Aisled Round-House Culture in the North', *P.P.S.* XIV, (1948), 46–125.

STEVENSON, R. B. K. 'The Nuclear Fort of Dalmahoy, Midlothian, and other Dark Age Capitals', *P.S.A.S.* LXXXIII (1948–49), 186–198.

— 'Pins and the Chronology of the Brochs', *P.P.S.,* XXI (1955), 282–94.

WAINWRIGHT, F. T. 'Souterrains in Scotland', *Antiquity* XXVII (1953), 219–32.

— 'Houses and Graves', in *P.P.*

— '*The Souterrains of Southern Pictland,* London, 1963.

WATSON, W. J. *The History of the Celtic Place-names of Scotland,* Edinburgh, 1926.

YOUNG, A. 'Brochs and Duns' *P.S.A.S.* XCV (1961–62), 171–98.

YOUNG, H. W. 'Notes on the Ramparts of Burghead as revealed by recent Excavations', *P.S.A.S.* XXV (1890–91), 435–447.

— 'Notes on Further Excavations at Burghead', *P.S.A.S.* XXVII. (1892–93), 86–91.

CHAPTERS II & IV

ANDERSON, A. O. *Early Sources of Scottish History, AD 500–1286,* 2 vols. Edinburgh, 1922.

ANDERSON, M. O. 'The Scottish Materials in a Paris Manuscript', *S.H.R.* XXVIII (1949), 31–42.

— 'The Lists of the Kings', *S.H.R.* XXVIII (1949), 108–18, XXIX (1950), 13–22.

ANNALS OF ULSTER, vol. I, ed. W. M. Hennessy, Dublin, 1887 (with English translation).

BEDE, *Historia Ecclesiastica Gentis Anglorum,* in *Baedae Opera Historica,* ed. C. Plummer, 2 vols., Oxford, 1896 (translation, Everyman's Library, by J. S. Stevens, revised by J. A. Giles).

BLAIR, P. HUNTER, 'The Bernicians and their Northern Frontier', in *Studies in Early British History,* ed. N. K. Chadwick, Cambridge, 1954.

CHADWICK, H. M. *Early Scotland,* Cambridge, 1949.

SKENE, W. F. *Chronicles of the Picts, Chronicles of the Scots, and other Early Memorials of Scottish History,* ed. W. F. Skene, Edinburgh, 1867.

— *Celtic Scotland,* vol. I, 2nd ed. Edinburgh, 1886.

WAINWRIGHT, F. T. 'Nechtanesmere', *Antiquity* XXII (1948), 82–97.

— 'The Picts and the Problem', in *P.P.*

— 'Picts and Scots', in *The Northern Isles,* ed. F. T. Wainwright, Edinburgh, 1962.

CHAPTER III

ANDERSON, A. O. and M. O. (eds) *Adomnan's Life of Columba,* Edinburgh, 1961.

BEDE, *Historia Ecclesiastica Gentis Anglorum,* in *Baedae Opera Historica,* ed. C. Plummer, 2 vols., Oxford, 1896.

BOWEN, E. G. *The Settlement of the Celtic Saints in Wales,* Cardiff, 1954.

CHADWICK, O. 'The Evidence of Dedications in the Early History of the Welsh Church', in *Studies in Early British History,* ed. N. K. Chadwick, Cambridge, 1954.

DONALDSON, G. 'Scottish Bishops' Sees before the Reign of David I', *P.S.A.S.* LXXXVII (1952–53), 106–117.

— and RADFORD, C. A. R. *Whithorn and Kirkmadrine,* Ministry of Works Official Guide-Book, Edinburgh, 1953.

DOWDEN, J. 'Notes on the True Date of the October Festival of St. Regulus...' *P.S.A.S.* XXVII (1892–3), 247–54.

DUKE, J. A. *The Columban Church,* Oxford, 1932, reprinted Edinburgh, 1957.

MACEWEN, A. R. *A History of the Church in Scotland,* vol. I, London, 1913.

MACKINLAY, J. M. *Ancient Church Dedications in Scotland*, vol. II, Non-Scriptural, Edinburgh, 1914.

MacQUEEN, J. *St. Nynia*, Edinburgh, 1961.

RADFORD, C. A. R. *The Early Christian and Norse Settlements at Birsay*, Orkney Ministry of Works Official Guide-Book, Edinburgh, 1959.

REEVES, W. (ed.) *Adamnan's Vita Sancti Columbae*, Dublin, 1857.

SIMPSON, W. D. *Saint Ninian and the Origins of the Christian Church in Scotland*, Edinburgh, 1940.

SKENE, W. F. *Celtic Scotland*, vol. II, 2nd ed. Edinburgh, 1887.

THOMPSON, E. A. 'The Origin of Christianity in Scotland', *S.H.R.* XXXVII, (1958) 17–22.

CHAPTER V

ALLEN, J. ROMILLY and ANDERSON, J. *The Early Christian Monuments of Scotland*, Edinburgh, 1903.

CRUDEN, STEWART, *The Early Christian and Pictish Monuments of Scotland*. An illustrated introduction with illustrated and descriptive catalogues of the Meigle and St Vigeans collections. *H.M.S.O.,* Edinburgh, 1964.

GORDON, C. A. 'Carving Technique on the Symbol Stones of North-East Scotland', *P.S.A.S.* LXXXVIII (1954–56), 40–46.

HENDERSON, I. 'The Origin Centre of the Pictish Symbol Stones', *P.S.A.S.* XCI (1957–58), 44–60.

MOWBRAY, CECIL L. (Mrs C. L. CURLE) 'Eastern Influences on Carvings at St Andrews and Nigg, Scotland', *Antiquity* X (1936), 428–440.

— 'The Chronology of the Early Christian Monuments of Scotland' *P.S.A.S.* LXXIV (1939–40), 60–116.

RADFORD, C. A. R. 'The Early Christian Monuments of Scotland', *Antiquity,* XVI (1942), 1–18.

— 'Two Scottish Shrines: Jedburgh and St Andrews', *A.J.* CXII (1955), 43–60.

STEVENSON, R. B. K. 'Pictish Art', in *P.P.*

— 'The Chronology and Relationships of some Irish and Scottish Crosses', *Journal of Royal Society of Antiquaries of Ireland,* LXXXVI, (1956), 84–96.

— 'The Inchyra Stone and Other Unpublished Early Christian Monuments', *P.S.A.S.* XCII (1958–59), 33–55 (with a summary of the various dating systems for Pictish sculpture put forward by a number of writers).

THOMAS, CHARLES. 'The Animal Art of the Scottish Iron Age and its Origins', *A.J.* CXVIII (1961), 14–64.

— 'The Interpretation of the Pictish Symbols', *A.J.* CXX (1963), 31–97.

Sources of Illustrations

Acknowledgement for photographs used in the plates is made to the following: Crown copyright, the Ministry of Public Building and Works including a number of photographs taken from the Ministry's illustrated guide book, *The Early Christian and Pictish Monuments of Scotland*, by Stewart Cruden, published by H.M. Stationary Office, 4–8, 11, 30, 39–43, 45, 46, 49, 52–59, 62–65; National Museum of Antiquities of Scotland, Edinburgh, 1, 16, 17, 18, 26–29, 34–36, 44, 47, 48, 50, 60, 61; Senatus Academicus, University of Aberdeen, 19–22, 25; Trustees of the British Museum, 2, 32, 51; Committee for Aerial Photography, University of Cambridge, 14, 15; Scottish National Portrait Gallery, Edinburgh, 3; Bibliothèque Nationale, Paris, 33; Mr Tom Weir, 9; John Leng & Co. Ltd, Dundee, 10; University of Edinburgh, 12; Valentine & Sons Ltd, 13; Perth Museum and Dundee Corporation Museums Dept, 24; The Master and Fellows of Corpus Christi College, Cambridge, 38; Mr J. R. Coull, 23; Kirkwall Town Council, 37; Society of Antiquaries of Scotland, 31.

THE PLATES

1

2

3

7

8

9

10

11

12

13

14

15

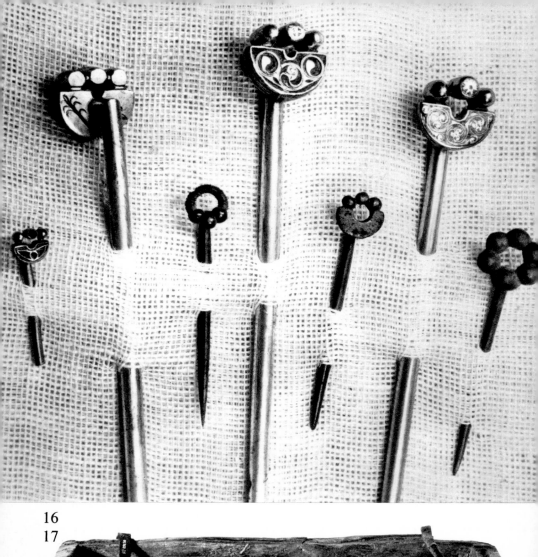

16
17

18

20

19

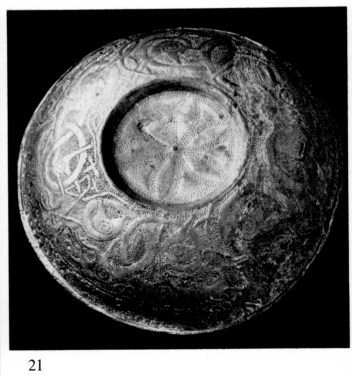

21

22

23

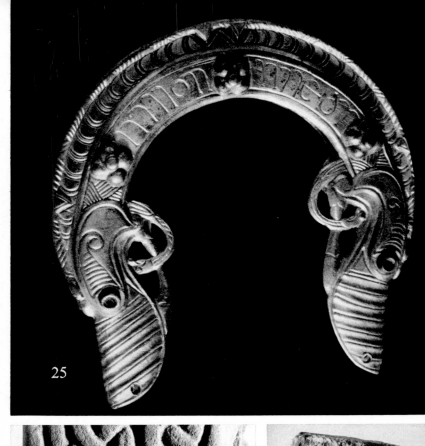

24

25

26

27

28   29

30   31

32

33

34

35

36

37

38

43

44

45

46

47

48

49

50

51

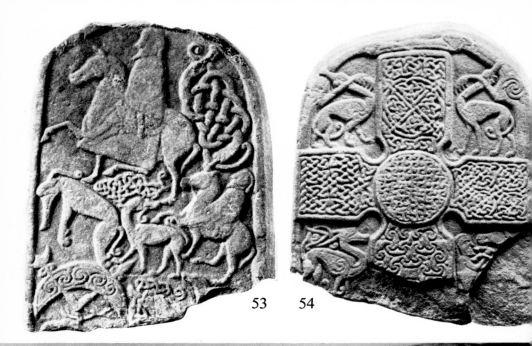

53   54

55

56   57

58

59

60

61

62

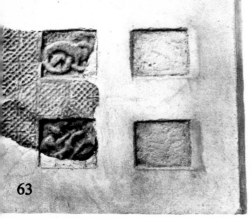

63

64

65

Notes on the Plates

1 Bridgeness Slab. Height 3 ft. National Museum of Antiquities of Scotland, Edinburgh. The left panel of a large commemorative slab from Bridgeness, Carriden, near the Forth, at the eastern end of the Antonine Wall. The sculpture preserves the appearance of the northern tribesmen as seen by a Roman cavalryman of the second century AD. His victims are lightly armed with rectangular shields, swords and spears but are otherwise naked.

2 Drawing of a Pict, John White (fl. 1577–93), British Museum, London. This Renaissance drawing illustrates well the picture of the Picts conjured up by Classical writers of the early centuries of our era. The impressive, if alien, figure of the Pict entirely covered with tattoo designs bears little relation to the primitive but entirely commonplace natives of the Bridgeness slab.

3 Detail from a wall painting in the National Portrait Gallery, Edinburgh, by William Hole (1846–1917) (cf. p. 45).

4 Interior of the Broch of Mousa, Shetland. This is the most complete of the brochs. It stands 43 ft 6 in. high and has a base diameter of 50 ft. The picture shows the dry-stone masonry, the projecting ridge which may have supported a verandah roof, and openings to galleries and staircases.

5 Interior of a wheel-house, Jarlshof, Shetland, showing hearth and compartments. Built from the second to the third century AD by newcomers to the Jarlshof site, whose descendants occupied the wheelhouses and huts of the post-broch period throughout the period of the historical Picts up to the time of the arrival of the Norse.

6 The *souterrain* and surface dwellings at Ardestie, Angus. This site shows a sequence of *souterrain* and post-*souterrain* occupation, the surface structures being used by historical Picts who were the descendants of the users of the *souterrain* (cf. p. 28).

7 Hadrian's Wall, view from Cuddy's Crag to the west of the Wall fort, Housesteads. The Wall was completed by about AD 127. Running for about seventy miles from Tyne to Solway it was equipped with forts, milecastles and turrets. The construction was of stone throughout and of the highest quality. The Wall remained an effective frontier, in spite of temporary destructions, until about the end of the fourth century.

8 Rough Castle, Bonnybridge, Stirlingshire, fort on the Antonine Wall. The photograph shows the turf work on the cobbling of the rampart foundation. The Antonine Wall, of turf construction, was completed by the General Lollius Urbicus for the emperor Antoninus Pius about AD 142. Of simpler design than Hadrian's Wall, it had no milecastles and turrets, but the distance between the wall forts was smaller. It ran for about forty miles between the Forth and the the Clyde estuaries. The date of its final occupation is not known exactly, but it had a much shorter life as a frontier defence than did the wall to the south, never recovering from a severe destruction round about AD 180.

9 View of Glen Lyon, Perthshire, from north-west across the Caledonian pinewood on the Allt Connait whose outlet is the loch west of Meggernie. The Perthshire glens and waterways formed the natural corridors between the kingdom of the Picts and the kingdom of the Scots, and must have been the scene of many skirmishes. The Pictish fort at Dundurn at the eastern end of Loch Earn was obviously sited to guard one of these points of entry to the Pictish kingdom.

10 The Mounth, the mountain range which separates Angus and Kincardineshire from Deeside. Although a clearly defined physical barrier, the Mounth is penetrated deeply by glens and there are many passes linking south with north (*cf.* p. 18). The photograph shows the top of Glen Esk, Angus.

11 The church of the Celtic monastery, Whithorn, Wigtownshire. This small dry-stone building lies just to the east of the ruins of the medieval cathedral. The outer face of its walls are daubed with white plaster and it has been suggested that this accounts for the tradition, recorded by Bede, that St Ninian's church was known as *Candida Casa,* 'the White House'.

However, the building may in fact belong to a somewhat later period in the history of the monastery (*cf.* p. 69).

12 *Vallum* of the Celtic monastery, Iona, Argyll, showing the bank of the monastic enclosure which belongs to the time of St Columba. The boat-shaped Viking grave inserted in the *vallum* dates from the period of repeated devastation of the Iona community and its buildings by the Norse, from the end of the eighth century onwards. The raids made it impossible for Iona to continue as the administrative centre of the Colum-ban Church.

13 Dunnottar Rock, Kincardineshire. Probably the site of *Dun Foither* which appears twice in the Irish *Annals* for the seventh century as having been under siege. On the rock of Dinnacair, to the immediate north of Dun-nottar, six symbol stones were found which have since been placed in the garden of Banchory House. The symbols are poorly executed and debased in design but are evidence for the use of the rocky promontories of this area by historical Picts.

14 Burghead, Moray Firth. The site of a timber-laced fort built in the true *Murus Gallicus* technique (*cf.* H. W. Young, *PSAS*, XXV (1890–91) and XXVII (1892–93). At Burghead were found numerous slabs with bulls incised upon them in a typically Pictish style (*cf.* Pl. 32). The promontory controls the entrance to the Moray Firth and was probably of importance at all periods. A few miles along the coast is the Sculptor's Cave, Covesea, with its rich evidence for Bronze Age settlement. The cave was used later, if only temporarily, in the Roman period (fourth century AD). Drawings on the walls of the cave include simplified ver-sions of the Pictish symbols but the excavation report does not make it clear whether there is any means of definitely relating their execution to either of the phases of occupation or whether they could equally well be the work of later squatters or sheltering fishermen (*cf.* Sylvia Benton, The Excavation of the Sculptor's Cave, Covesea, Morayshire, *PSAS* LXV, (1930–31), 177–216

15 Tap o' Noth, Huntly, Aberdeenshire. Length 345 ft, width 126 ft. A vitrified fort of unusual size. *Cf.* David Christison, *Early Fortifications in Scotland,* Edinburgh, 1898.

16 Silver 'hand-pins', bearing Pictish symbols, including an example from Norrie's Law, Largo, Fife. National Museum of Antiquities of Scotland, Edinburgh. Opinions vary concerning the chronology of these and related pins. It has been shown how the simple ringheaded pin developed in the third and fourth centuries to a ring with beads on the upper curve which in turn straightened out to produce the hand-pin proper. R.B.K. Stevenson dates the hand-pins to the seventh century but Mrs Fowler suggests a fifth- or sixth-century date. The symbol-bearing hand-pin, one of a pair, comes from the Norrie's Law hoard; the date of the deposition of the hoard is, however, also disputed. *Cf.* R.B.K. Stevenson, 'Pins and the Chronology of the Brochs', *PPS* XXI, 1955, Elizabeth Fowler, 'Celtic Metalwork of Fifth and Sixth Centuries AD', *A.J.* CXX, 1963.

17 Carved wooden box, Birsay, Orkney. National Museum of Antiquities of Scotland, Edinburgh. The box, which is almost 12 in. long, has been dated to between the eighth and tenth centuries. It is the only surviving piece of wood carving of the period and it has been suggested that the tools it contains might be those of a leather worker. The box is therefore a useful reminder of the lost products of the wood-carver and leather-worker which may have contained many clues as to the influences at work on Pictish art.

18 Silver chain, Whitecleuch, Lanarkshire; silver plaque, Norrie's Law, Largo, Fife; silver penannular brooch, Tummel Bridge, Perthshire. All at National Museum of Antiquities of Scotland, Edinburgh. Ten of these massive double-linked silver chains have been found, only three in sites north of the Forth-Clyde line, but the rest almost certainly having been taken to the south as booty. The characteristic Pictish symbols on the surviving terminal rings associate the chains firmly with the Picts. Analysis of the silver used for one of the chains suggests that they were made from melted-down silver gilt of the Roman period. An opening in the terminal ring allows the passage of single links by manipulation so that when all four links at the ends of the chain are in the ring the chain is securely fastened. The use to which the chains were put is unknown but they were probably neck ornaments. The engraving of the symbols on the fastening rings and on the Norrie's Law plaque is of exquisite

quality and the design of the symbols is complex. They belong, there⁄ fore, to the classic period of the symbolism represented by the early Class I sculptured stones. The function of the plaque, one of a pair, is not known, and the date of the hoard of which it is part, is as we have seen, debated. The silver brooch is one of three found in a Perthshire hoard along with hanging⁄bowl fragments datable to the fifth or sixth century. Recent analysis of this type of brooch has suggested that the type originated in Scotland and has a date span of mid⁄fifth to eighth century with the Tummel Bridge examples standing near the beginning of the series. *Cf.* Elizabeth Fowler, *op. cit.* Others however, suggest a seventh⁄ to eighth⁄ century date for the brooches. It is perhaps worth noting that while the chains with their symbol⁄bearing rings are unique to the Picts in the way that the symbol stones are, the penannular brooch belongs equally to the repertoire of Irish and British metalworkers. It is perhaps not surprising, therefore, that so far no symbol⁄bearing brooch has turned up. In this connection the Norrie's Law hand⁄pin is exceptional, and the somewhat broken⁄down version of the symbols engraved there may be of significance.

19 Silver spoon, St Ninian's Isle, Shetland. Length 8 in. Now with the rest of the St Ninian's Isle treasure in the National Museum of Antiquities of Scotland, Edinburgh. This is the only native spoon in the British Isles datable to the eighth century. It was evidently hung up by its looped end and its delicate construction indicates that it was never intended for regular use at table. It is thought to be a liturgical spoon, perhaps for holding oil. (*Cf.* Pl. 22.)

20 Conical mounting, St Ninian's Isle treasure. Height 1¾ in. One of three similar silver objects originally heavily gilded. It is not known how it was used but details of construction suggest that it was fitted to some object by leather thongs. The roll of the hindquarters of the entwined animals is very similar to that of the animals on the right panel of the cross side of the Aberlemno Churchyard stone – themselves highly rem⁄ iniscent of certain Lindisfarne animals. These animals seem to share with Aberlemno the 'ball and claw' feet which are characteristic of Pictish art.

21 Silver bowl, St Ninian's Isle treasure. Approx. diameter 5½ in. Seven silver bowls were found in the treasure. With the exception of the Orm⁄

side bowl, no comparable native silver bowls have been found in this country. R.B.K. Stevenson has pointed out parallels in the design and technique of the bowls with the Monymusk Reliquary, sufficiently close to suggest that they came from the same workshop. The hindquarters of the intertwined animals are again treated in the Lindisfarne-Aberlemno manner and the dog-like faces are also to be found among the animals of the decorated pages of the Lindisfarne Gospels.

22   Silver one-pronged implement, St Ninian's Isle treasure. Length 6½ in. This object is unparalleled. Like the spoon it has a suspension ring. The prong has a cutting edge and it has been suggested that it was used for cutting and picking up the Host. It probably belongs with the spoon as part of the church plate of a Pictish church.

23   St Ninian's Isle, Shetland. Excavations conducted between 1955 and 1959 uncovered the medieval church on the island. Underneath the foundations were discovered the ruins of a pre-Norse church which therefore belongs to the period of the historical Picts. Seven post stones of what has been identified by Mr C.A.R. Radford as part of a Founder's Tomb were found to the south of the medieval apse. The incised symbols on the posts are generally described as Pictish, but they are spirals, cups and sea-horses; while undoubtedly related to the Pictish symbols in manner, these are not in fact examples of true symbols. The hoard was found in 1958 at what can be deduced as the floor level of the Pictish church. It was in a wooden box buried upside down as though in haste. The most plausible explanation offered for the somewhat miscellaneous nature of the hoard is that it represented the movable wealth of the foundation and so included gifts from the community it served. This would account, for example, for the large number of brooches. For discussion of the treasure, see 'The Ninian's Isle Silver Hoard', *Antiquity* XXXIII, 1959. 'Saint Ninian's Isle Treasure', *Aberdeen University Studies* No. 141 is an excellent photographic record by Alexander Cain with notes by Professor A.C. O'Dell who conducted the excavation.

24   Ogam inscription, Inchyra, Perthshire. Height 5 ft 3 in. Perth Museum. The majority of the Pictish inscriptions are written in the Ogam alphabet (*cf.* p. 31 above). The main inscription of a number on the Inchyra

stone is shown. F. T. Wainwright's tentative transliteration is as follows: INEHHETESTIETD. No interpretation of the inscription, which may continue along the top edge of the stone, has been suggested. The Inchyra stone is of considerable interest both for the number of its ogams and for the fact that it appears to have been used as a symbol stone on three successive occasions. *Cf.* F. T. Wainwright, *The Inchyra Ogam,* Dundee Archaeological Studies 1, R. B. K. Stevenson, *PSAS* XCII, 1958–59.

25   Silver mounting, St Ninian's Isle treasure. Height of horseshoe 3 in. Both sides of this silver object, which may be a scabbard chape, are inscribed. On the ornate side is written in majuscules, IN NOMINE D(EI) S(UMMI). 'In the name of God the Highest', and on the back in minuscules the owner's name, 'Resad, son of Spussico'. For these readings see Kenneth Jackson, 'The St Ninian's Isle Inscription: A Re-appraisal', *Antiquity* XXXIV, 1960.

26   St Vigeans, Angus. Detail of St Vigeans 1 now in the Museum at St Vigeans. The miniscule inscription reads: drosten/ipeuoret/ettfor/cus. *Drosten, Uoret* and *Forcus* are names. *Ett* is presumably Latin *et. Ipe* cannot be translated and belongs, presumably, to the unknown language of the Picts. The inscription is certainly contemporary with the carving, a point often in doubt with the ogams on symbol stones. The bottom of one of the edges is a curious place to put the inscription if the monument commemorates the three individuals named. The inscription can scarcely represent the sculptors' names, so it must be supposed that the habit of placing ogam inscriptions along the edge of stones has influenced the choice of position.

27   Inscription stone, Tarbet, Ross-shire. Height about 1 ft 6 in. Now in the National Museum of Antiquities of Scotland, Edinburgh. The inscription is written in Hiberno-Saxon majuscules of the eighth-ninth century. Romilly Allen gives the reading: IN NOMINE/IHESU CHRISTI/CRUX CHRISTI/IN COMMEMORATIONE/REO (TE)TII/REQUIESC (IT). No patently Christian commemoration of this type is found on any of the symbol-bearing stones.

28 Symbol stone, Dunnichen, Angus. Height 4 ft 8 in. J. Romilly Allen, *The Early Christian Monuments of Scotland,* Part III, 1903, p. 206. This stone was found on the margin of the marshy ground identified as Nech‑ton's Mere, the site of the important Pictish victory against the Northum‑brians in AD 685 (*cf.* p. 56 above). It is now in the garden of Dunnichen House. The symbols are deeply incised so that the area between the lines appears emergent resulting in a pseudo‑relief.

29 Symbol stone, South Ronaldsay, Orkney. Height 5 ft. Sandstone. *ECMS,* p. 20. National Museum of Antiquities of Scotland, Edinburgh. The stone is carved on both faces. The high quality of design and execution is typical of the Class I stones in the far north.

30 Manse stone, Glamis, Angus. Sandstone. Height 8 ft 9 in. In the manse garden near the church. *ECMS,* p. 221. There is a very similar monu‑ment half a mile to the south‑east of the church. The stone is carved on two faces. This side with incised symbols may have been executed some time before the relief cross and other designs, partly incised and partly in relief, found on the other side, but not necessarily so (*cf.* Pl. 39).

31 Symbol stone, Golspie, Sutherland. Sandstone. Height 4 ft 3¾ in. J. M. Davidson, 'A Pictish Symbol Stone from Golspie, Sutherland'. *PSAS* LXXVII, 1942–43, pp. 26–30. The stone, found in a field near Golspie and forming the cover‑stone of a cist, is now in Dunrobin Museum, Sutherland. This is perhaps the finest example of a Class I symbol stone. The in‑filling of the crescent has been shown to be the most complex pelta design used to decorate a crescent and the example of the Pictish beast holds a similar priority in the completeness of the details portrayed. The incision is extremely delicate giving the effect of a flowing and sensitive line drawing. It has been suggested that the incision could have been made, not with a chisel as is normal, but with the rounded point of a small nail.

32 Incised stone, Burghead, Moray. Sandstone. Height 1 ft 9 in. The stone, found in connection with harbour improvements, is now in the British Museum. One of a number of incised bulls found at Burghead (*cf.* Pl. 14). The Burghead bulls are exceptional in that they appear alone on small

slabs and in the number of representations found at the same site. Note how well the interior scrolls are used to articulate the muscles of the animal in comparison with the ineffective use of this convention by the artist of the Lion of St Mark in the Book of Durrow.

33 Echternach Gospels, Paris, Bibliothèque Nationale, Cod. Lat. 9389, fol. 115 vo. Symbol of St Luke. At the beginning of the eighth century, Willibrord, a Northumbrian churchman, founded a monastery at Echternach (Luxembourg) as part of his mission to the Frisians. The house became an important English missionary centre. The most celebrated product of its scriptorium is the Echternach Gospel book. It cannot be dated directly but a closely related manuscript, also from Echternach, belongs to the years between 703 and 721. The Gospels are therefore more or less contemporary with the Lindisfarne Gospels, although they have closer iconographical links with the Book of Durrow.

34 Incised stone, Grantown, Morayshire, Schist. Height 4 ft. *ECMS,* p. 126, National Museum of Antiquities of Scotland, Edinburgh.

35 Incised stone, Easterton of Roseisle, Morayshire. Sandstone. Height 4 ft. *ECMS.* p. 124. Found on a site three miles south-east of Burghead. The stone is now in the National Museum of Antiquities of Scotland, Edinburgh.

36 Fragment of an incised sculpture of a boar. Dores, Inverness-shire. *ECMS,* p. 97. Diorite. Height 1 ft 10 in. National Museum of Antiquities of Scotland, Edinburgh.

37 Detail of the symbol stone, Knowe of Burrian, Birsay, Orkney. In store at Sandness House, Kirkwall.

38 Gospels fragment, Cambridge, Corpus Christi College MS. 1976, English, eighth century. The closeness of the eagle design to that in the previous plate suggests that the manuscript must have been produced in a centre in some way exposed to Pictish influence, as, judging from the St Luke symbol, might also be the case with the Echternach Gospels.

39 Cross slab, Glamis, Angus. Sandstone. Height 8 ft 9 in. (*cf.* Pl. 30). Detail of the cross face. An early example of Pictish relief sculpture, and indeed in certain portions actually marking the transition from the incised to the relief technique. The cross has a pattern-filled circle at the joining of the four arms, as has also the cross on a slab at Rossie Priory, 12 miles away. The centaur and the beast on either side of the upper arm of the cross are evidently mere space-fillers, nevertheless the effect of the whole design is admirably unfussy and dignified. There is a strength and clarity in the use of line on both sides of the Glamis stone which makes it representative of Pictish art at its best.

40 Cross slab, Aberlemno, Angus. Sandstone. Height 7 ft 6 in. *ECMS* p. 209. The stone stands in Aberlemno churchyard. This monumental design belongs to exactly the same stage in the evolution of the Hiberno-Saxon style as the great Lindisfarne Gospels, with the same happy juxt-aposition of vigorous breadth and minute complexity. The vitality of the handling of the tangled beasts, and the presence of the sea-horses, a motif unparalleled in the great Gospel book, suggests that the art-style practised in Northumbria around AD 700 was perfectly comprehended beyond Northumbria to the North. The interlace pattern on the lower arm of the cross has been analyzed in *ECMS* II, p. 296. Allen sums up in the fol-lowing words: 'It is clear, therefore, that notwithstanding the apparent complication of the arrangement of cords, the design was not arrived at by any haphazard method, but was all carefully thought out beforehand. This may fairly lay claim to be the most elaborate interlaced pattern in sculptured stonework that has come down to us'. The elongated spiral-bodied animals at the left of the lower arm of the cross display the ball-and-claw foot characteristic of the Pictish sculpture.

41 Reverse of Aberlemno cross slab (Pl. 40). A mixture of relief and incised sculpture, similar to that found on the cross face of the Glamis manse slab. In the main area of relief sculpture, spears, bridles, and a sword are represented by incised lines. Dominated by two great symbols and framed at the sides by a border terminating at the apex of the stone with the confronted heads of two savage beasts, the rectangular relief displays what appears to be a single scene, a battlefield with various opposing soldiers, mounted and unmounted. In the right-hand bottom corner a dead war-

rior wearing a hauberk and a helmet with a nasal guard has fallen beside his shield and is pecked at by a carrion-bird.

This truly pictorial and narrative sculpture is unique in Pictish art, and is an outstanding example from the early Middle Ages of secular subject matter in art.

42 Cross slab, Eassie, Angus. Sandstone. Height 6 ft 8 in. *ECMS* p. 218. Situated in the churchyard at Eassie, between Meigle and Glamis. The cross has accomplished interlace patterns on its upper and side arms akin to those on the Glamis manse slab. The shaft has circular panels of inter-lace which relate the sculpture to Meigle 1. See *ECMS* II, p. 296.

Alongside the cross-shaft are stationed angels, or rather seraphim, with spirals on the wings reminiscent of the attendant angels on the Athlone gilt-bronze plaque of the Crucifixion in the National Museum, Dublin. The thin striding warrior with his oddly demoniac air, carries a spear and a rectangular shield like the man at the bottom centre of the St Andrews Sarcophagus.

43 Reverse of Eassie cross slab (Pl. 42). The meaning of the scene portrayed is unknown. The sculpture of the human figures and of the tree is notably less accomplished than that of the fine, pacing cattle.

44 Cross slab, Fowlis Wester, Perthshire. Sandstone. Height 5 ft 2 in. J. J. Waddell, 'Cross Slabs recently discovered at Fowlis Wester and Mill-port', *PSAS* LXVI, pp. 409–412. SS. Paul and Anthony, the famous hermit saints, or at least two seated clerics, face one another across the cross-shaft, the figure on the left being depicted in a forest setting, with formalized trees (*cf.* p. 148 above). The grotesque scenes at the top of the slab evidently include a reference to the spewing forth of Jonah by the whale.

45 Cross slab, St Vigeans 7, Angus. Sandstone. Height 5 ft 6 in. *ECMS* p. 268. St Vigeans Museum. The arms of the cross meet at a central richly interlaced medallion, as in the Glamis manse stone. The icono-graphy of the stone resembles that of Fowlis Wester, but in addition to SS. Paul and Anthony we have two curious representations of pagan rites, the adoration or sacrifice of a bull and a man held upside down

with his head on a block or in a cauldron. The imagery probably had no significance for the sculptor beyond its artistic form.

46 Meigle 26, Perthshire. Sandstone. Length 5 ft. *ECMS* p. 303. Ministry of Works Museum, Meigle. Detail of the recumbent grave-slab. The slab is carved on the top and the two long and two short sides. The central group in the procession of horsemen illustrated here is portrayed in depth; they appear one beyond the other, with a single smaller horseman, as if further off – a lively and picturesque effect which shows the sculptor exploiting very fully the aesthetic possibilities of shallow relief sculpture.

47 Cross slab, Woodwray, Angus. Sandstone. Height 5 ft 9 in. *ECMS* p. 242. Found in the foundations of the castle at Woodwray, two miles north of Aberlemno and now preserved in the National Museum of Antiquities, Edinburgh. The stone displays a selection of the monstrous animal forms which characterize this phase of Pictish art.

48 Cross slab, Dunfallandy, Perthshire. Sandstone. Height 5 ft. *ECMS*, p. 286. Situated at Dunfallandy, 2 miles south-east of Pitlochry, but earlier in a chapel near Killiecrankie. The relief sculpture on the back is framed by two wolf-faced, fish-tailed monsters, whose outstretched tongues lick a man's head at the apex of the slab, taking further the framing principle which we see in the Aberlemno battle scene. The large cross on the front is decorated with emergent bosses. The cross is accompanied on either side by fantastic animals, typical specimens from the Pictish 'Bestiary', like those at Woodwray.

49 Cross slab, St Vigeans, Forfarshire. Sandstone. Height 5 ft. *ECMS*, p. 235. St Vigeans Museum, (cf. Pl. 52 above). On each side of the cross are grotesque monsters of variegated form seen from contrasting viewpoints.

50 Grave-stone, Brough of Birsay, Orkney. Sandstone. Height 7 ft. National Museum of Antiquities, Edinburgh. Detail of the relief sculpture of three soldiers armed with spears and square shields. The leading figure in this Assyrian-like frieze is more handsomely equipped than the others. The stone was found in fragments at the west end of a triple grave. The suggestion

that the three occupants of the grave were actually the three soldiers carved on the stone is perhaps less improbable than that there should be some direct equation between the three sculptured soldiers and the four sculptured symbols above them.

For the triple burial, see C. A. R. Radford, *The Early Christian and Norse Settlements at Birsay, Orkney,* ed. C. A. Ralegh Radford, 1959, Edinburgh, p. 17.

51   Franks Casket. Whalebone. Length 9 in., breadth 7½ in. British Museum, London, except for one panel in the National Museum, Florence. Probably made in Northumbria around AD 700. The wolf in the Romulus and Remus scene illustrated, and the horse on the Florence panel, are reminiscent of Pictish incised animal designs, and the secular tone and iconography of the Franks Casket provides us with one of the few parallels to the Aberlemno battle scene. The casket may represent the kind of small portable object which could account for the interaction of art styles between Northumbria and the Pictish area.

52   Incised stone, St Vigeans 1, Angus. Sandstone. Height of complete stone 3 ft 7 in. (*cf*. Pl. 26 and 49). The decoration, apart from the three symbols, consists of naturalistic animals represented on various scales. None of these animal motifs appears to have any specific connection with any of the others. They look as if they had been lifted from a model-book of stereotype designs. Some, such as the doe suckling its young, are designs of impressive antiquity. The archer-figure occurs on a number of Class II stones.

53   Cross slab, Meigle 4, Perthshire. Sandstone. Height 5 ft, whole. Meigle Museum. The top of this slab contains horsemen, animals and Pictish symbols in close juxtaposition. Interwoven between them are elaborately enmeshed serpents whose graceful and complex involutions come close to the Anglo-Danish Urnes style.

54   Meigle 4, cross side. The animals flanking the upper arm of the cross have the same elegance as those at Dunfallandy. The borders transformed into animals at the apex of the stone provide a motif found regularly in the relief slabs.

55   Detail of stone slab, Meigle 26, Perth. Sandstone. Length of complete stone 5 ft. A spectacular monster whose tail is intertwined with a serpent, a design conceived in the same spirit as the matted serpents in Pl. 53.

56, 57   Cross slab, Meigle 2, Perth. Sandstone. Height 8 ft 1 in. *ECMS*, p. 297. Meigle Museum. A monumental cross slab, now much weathered but still extraordinarily impressive in its rich plasticity and scale. The complex grotesque creatures flanking the cross shaft recall St Vigeans 1. On the reverse one is very aware of the artist's use of Mediterranean models. The scale and the spirit of the sculpture has an essential classicism and grandeur which shows how completely he understood his models.

58, 59   Cross slab, Aberlemno Roadside, Angus. Sandstone. Height 9 ft 3 in. *ECMS*, p. 214. A great cross slab of unusual restraint and soberness of imagery. Two angels appear to mourn with drooping wings on either side of the cross, a contrast to the grotesqueries of the Pictish 'Bestiary' normally placed in this position. In mood, the monument anticipates Romanesque art.

    The reverse shows the scaling-up of the symbols which characterizes the late phase of Pictish art. The hunting scene was evidently worked by an artist familiar with the Hilton of Cadboll stone or its model (see Pl. 60). At the very bottom is a pictorial allusion to David.

60   Cross slab, Hilton of Cadboll, Ross-shire. Sandstone. Height 7 ft 9 in. *EMCS*, p. 61. National Museum of Antiquities, Edinburgh. The cross side of the monument is obliterated. On the upper half of the reverse, three colossal symbols show the complete abandonment of the traditional infilling patterns. The central portion shows a typical hunting scene, made notable by the female rider and by the trumpeters who accompany her (*cf.* p. 154 above). The loose-trumpet-spiral below the hunting scene and the scraggy pattern of foliage and birds in the borders is brittle and sophisticated in exactly the manner associated with Mercian art around AD 800.

61   Cross slab, Nigg, Ross-shire. Sandstone. Height 7 ft 9 in. *ECMS*, p. 61. Nigg churchyard. The sumptuous cross is bordered by the most impressive example of boss sculpture in the Pictish area. Fat snakes encircle

bosses carved with tightly knitted interlace. The technical skill involved is of the highest order. The Nigg stone is one of the greatest expositions of the abstract art-style of the Hiberno-Saxon school. The figure sculpture of SS. Anthony and Paul at the apex of the stone provides a sculptural parallel to the figure-drawing in the Book of Kells (*cf.* p. 156 above). The reverse bears David imagery much mutilated.

62–64   The St Andrew Sarcophagus, St. Andrews, Fife. Sandstone. Length, as reconstructed, 5 ft 9 in., height 2 ft 4 in. to base of the sloping roof. On the reconstruction, see C. A. Ralegh Radford, *Archaeological Journal* CXII, 1955, pp. 43–60. The side panels which flank the main sculptured panel are stylistically akin to the Nigg stone (Pl. 61) in their quality of relief and the subtlety of their contrasting textures. The cruciform end-panels reveal the close connection with the cross slabs. The central panel combines a majestic classicism in its main figure of David with a romantic lyrical mood in the figures and animals invading the zone of tangled foliage at the left. The sarcophagus is a major work of European art, a Pictish contribution to the Carolingian *renovatio*.

65   Maiden Stone, Chapel of Garioch, Aberdeenshire. Red granite. Height 10 ft. Situated one mile west of the Chapel of Garioch on the northern slope of the Mither Tap, Aberdeenshire. This massive monument with its ponderous symbols well suited to grandiloquent, almost flaunting, display of the Pictish symbolism evident on the monuments just prior to its disappearance.

Index